To. Pastor Hughes

Aug.ᵗ 1942.

12/6

THE SPIRIT OF METHODISM

THE
SPIRIT OF METHODISM

BY

HENRY BETT
M.A., Litt.D.

Published for the
FERNLEY-HARTLEY TRUST

THE EPWORTH PRESS
(EDGAR C. BARTON)
25–35 City Road, London, E.C.1

Made in Great Britain

CONTENTS

TO
WILLIAM FREDERICK
LOFTHOUSE

Chapter I

THE RELIGIOUS EXPERIENCE OF JOHN WESLEY

In the whole history of the Church of Christ there has never been a more remarkable movement than Methodism or a more remarkable man than John Wesley,[1] and the man and the movement are singularly identified. Methodism owed much to Charles Wesley and to George Whitefield, and it would have been a different story if the revival had lacked the impulse of Whitefield's amazing oratory in the earliest days, and the inspiration of Charles Wesley's wonderful hymns all through its history. Nevertheless, it is John Wesley who stands out from the beginning of the work to the end of his life as, by the grace of God, the creative spirit and the dominant personality of the Evangelical Revival.[2] His great gifts of mind and spirit, his strength of purpose, his organizing ability, and his incredible industry, all dedicated from day to day to the highest and holiest service, and marvellously used by the Spirit of God – all these made him the

[1] An Arbeitskraft und Arbeitsleistung sind wenige Menschen ihm gleich gewesen, an Vielseitigkeit der Bildung und nie erlahmendem Wissensinteresse sucht er unter den Erweckungspredigern aller Zeiten seines Gleichen. - Loofs, ' Methodismus ', in Herzog-Hauck *Realencyklopädie für protestantische Theologie und Kirche*, Heft 119, p. 781.

[2] Discussing the share of John Wesley, Charles Wesley, and Whitefield in the movement, M. Augustin Leger remarks, ' Mais, à le prendre tout entier, John est indiscutablement le plus complet ; poète, orateur, régulateur de croyances et meneur d'hommes, il rassemble et il résume, dans sa chétive personne, les caractères distinctifs de cette renaissance religieuse. Qui la veut étudier dans une de ses incarnations particulières, ne saurait mieux s'addresser qu' à lui'. – *La Jeunesse de Wesley*, p. xix.

Apostle of England. If that title sounds extravagant, it should be remembered that as a mere matter of fact no Englishman has ever lived, from the time when Augustine landed in Kent to the present day, who led so many of the people of this land from a life of sin and selfishness and worldliness into the knowledge and the service of God. Wesley himself remarked, in 1785, that the number of those who had been brought to God in the Methodist revival of religion was perhaps greater than in any other age since the times of the Apostles, and the statement can hardly be challenged by anyone who knows anything of the facts.

Within a few months from now there will be widespread celebrations of the bi-centenary of Methodism. In these two hundred years the largest evangelical community in the world has come into existence, and spread into every land, so that to-day there are probably some fifty millions of people who belong to it, by more or less intimate association. The significance of this stands out for all to see. There has never been, since the first age of Christianity, any evangelistic movement so rapid, so widespread, and so colossal in its results. Upon any estimate which accepts the reality of religion at all it is the greatest work of the Spirit of God in the history of the Church.

This great movement is unique in many senses, and very strikingly in this – that it stands in the most intimate connexion with the religious experience of one man. John Wesley meant more to Methodism than perhaps any other religious leader ever did to any other religious movement. There have been periods in the past where we feel, as we look back, that a religious revival was in the air at the time, and where it is at least possible to think that other men than the actual leaders might have been the protagonists. If St. Francis had never lived there was St. Dominic, and if Luther had never lived there was Calvin. But it is scarcely conceivable that any other Englishman in the middle of the eighteenth century could have done what Wesley did. No one else could possibly have been, in the way that Wesley was, the origin, the centre, and the momentum of the movement. Methodism was not only dominated for fifty years by his personality, but in the providence of God it sprang from what happened, first of all, in his own spiritual life. For several centuries past Christendom has not produced any man whose religious experience is more worthy of intimate study. Perhaps he is the only man in the modern world whose spiritual history deserves, alike for its innate interest and for its importance in the life of the Church, to be named beside that of Luther, of St. Augustine, and of St. Paul himself.

Every one who studies Wesley's experience before 1738 will learn to look upon those years as an era of preliminary discipline. However we regard what happened in May 1738, it is a fact that it marked the profoundest cleavage in Wesley's experience. It was the greatest crisis in his religious life. All that went before led up to it. That fact being recognized, we are next impressed by the remarkable complexity of the experience that constituted this spiritual preparation. Probably no Englishman of the eighteenth century lived so varied a life as Wesley, and probably no religious leader ever passed through a wider range of experiences and emotions than Wesley did in his earlier years. Let us try to disentangle some of the significant facts and influences in his early religious life.

His ancestry is noteworthy, for both his grandfathers and one great-grandfather were ejected ministers in 1662. Though his father and mother had conformed, there was a freer strain in their blood. The Epworth household represented the English Church of the eighteenth century at its best. The Rector of Epworth was emphatically a devout man, though rugged in character and deficient in evangelical experience. Susanna Wesley was one of the best of mothers, a woman of strong and spiritual mind, exceptionally well educated for her century, a lover of Pascal and George Herbert, resolute and yet gentle, singularly wise in her counsels to her children, and greatly beloved by them.

The famous fire at the Rectory in 1709, when John Wesley, as a child of nearly six, was snatched from death, certainly counted in his spiritual development. He remembered it vividly all his life. On February 9, 1750, he records in his *Journal*, ' About eleven o'clock it came into my mind ' (he was holding a Watchnight Service in West Street Chapel in London) ' that this was the very day and hour on which forty years ago [*sic*] I was taken out of the flames. I stopped and gave a short account of that wonderful providence'. When Wesley was seriously ill late in 1753, and thought he was likely to die, he made the famous entry in his *Journal*, on November 26, ' In the evening (not knowing how it might please God to dispose of me) to prevent vile panegyric, I wrote as follows : " Here lieth the body of John Wesley, a brand plucked out of the burning : who died of a consumption in the fifty-first year of his age, not leaving, after his debts are paid, ten pounds behind him ; praying God be merciful to me, an unprofitable servant ! " He ordered that this, if any, inscription should be placed upon his tombstone.' Charles Wesley quotes this in his *Journal*, under the date December 2, but makes the phrase run, ' A brand, *not once only*, plucked out of

the fire '.   Beneath an early portrait of John Wesley
there was a vignette of the blazing house, with the
motto, ' Is not this a brand plucked out of the
fire ? '   All his life long John Wesley had the feeling
that in this escape he had been remarkably spared
for some special purpose.   His mother felt it too,
and recorded the resolve, two years after the fire:
' I do intend to be more particularly careful of the
soul of this child, that Thou hast so mercifully provided for, than ever I have been, that I may do my
endeavour to instil into his mind the principles of
true religion and virtue.   Lord, give me grace to
do it sincerely and prudently, and bless my attempts
with good success ! '   It is significant that his
father admitted the boy to the Lord's Table when
he was only eight years old.

In 1714, in his eleventh year, the little fellow was
sent to the Charterhouse.   Writing in 1738, he
says of his schooldays: ' Outward restraints being
removed, I was . . . almost continually guilty of
outward sins, which I knew to be such, though they
were not scandalous in the eye of the world.'   This
must be interpreted with reserve.   He was always
severe upon himself, and he was always much too
adult in his judgements upon childhood ; moreover,
he was writing in the first flush of a deepened experience.   He goes on to make it clear that as a
schoolboy he regularly read the Bible and said his
prayers.   ' However, I still read the Scriptures, and
said my prayers, morning and evening.   And what
I now hoped to be saved by was, (1) not being so
bad as other people ; (2) having still a kindness for
religion ; and (3) reading the Bible, going to
Church, and saying my prayers.'   It is plain that,
though he must have missed his mother's influence
and the discipline of the home at Epworth, and
though the child's nature probably coarsened

somewhat in the life of an eighteenth-century public school, he was still a pure and honourable boy of devout habits.

He went to Oxford in 1720, at the age of seventeen. Oxford was unquestionably at that time the most demoralized and demoralizing university in Europe. The descriptions of contemporary life at Oxford by Edward Gibbon and Adam Smith are well known. They witness that even the pretence of teaching was given up, for the most part, by the professors and lecturers ; that the students wasted their time in drinking and gambling ; and that in the matter of religion generally the University (in the phrase of the great historian) ' had contrived to unite the opposite extremes of bigotry and indifference '. Wesley's character does not appear to have suffered, however, while he was at Oxford. During the whole of his undergraduate career he was a sprightly youth, the life of every company in which he found himself, gay and sociable, but blameless in behaviour. Let it be said emphatically, in despite of what some have suggested, that there is no sign whatever of any moral degeneracy in Wesley's early life at Oxford. At Epworth he had been under the eye of his parents : at the Charterhouse he had been more or less under the tutelage of his brother Samuel, who was Usher at Westminster. When he went to Oxford he was more his own master than ever he had been in his life. He found it difficult to be as economical as perhaps he ought to have been, remembering the *res angusta domi*. But this was all. At Oxford, as all his life long, judged by the ordinary standards, he was a blameless character.[1] But his spiritual sensibilities

[1] Ayant dégagé de notre mieux la jeunesse de Wesley des lourdes accusations que certains de ses disciples ont tenu à articuler pour lui donner matière à conversion, nous croyons pouvoir conclure que ni au collège de

were not yet aroused ; his soul still slept. 'I had not all this while so much as a notion of inward holiness,' he writes in his *Journal*.

The first awakening came in 1725. It seems to have been directly connected with the choice of a vocation. He had taken his bachelor's degree in 1724. 'When I was about twenty-two,' he wrote afterward, ' my father pressed me to enter into holy orders.' The definite emergence of the Christian ministry as a possible career made him begin to ask if he were fit for it. The result was a deepened seriousness and a considerable change in his life. On February 23, 1725, his mother wrote : ' The alteration of your temper has occasioned me much speculation. I, who am apt to be sanguine, hope it may proceed from the operations of God's Holy Spirit.'

It is characteristic of the scholar in Wesley that books contributed considerably to the change. ' At the same time, the providence of God directing me to Kempis's *Christian Pattern*, I began to see that true religion was seated in the heart, and that God's law extended to all our thoughts as well as words and actions. I was, however, very angry at Kempis for being too strict ; though I read him only in Dean Stanhope's translation.' At the same period he read Jeremy Taylor's *Holy Living and Dying*, and, on his mother's recommendation, Scougal's *Life of God in the Soul of Man*. The main result of his study of Jeremy Taylor was that he became more careful in his use of time, and began to keep detailed diaries in consequence. It is significant that even then he

Londres, ni pendant les cinq premières années d'université, John Wesley ne se distingua de ses compagnons soit par une piété plus expansive, soit par une vie de péchés. S'il resta toujours fidèle à ses devoirs religieux élémentaires, il ne recherchait pas les exercices surérogatoires ; d'autre part, s'il s'accuse vaguement d'avoir péché, on a tort d'interpréter trop littéralement ces déclarations de converti. – Piette, *La Réaction Wesléyenne dans l'Évolution Protestante*, p. 361. The reference to ' lourdes accusations ' is to Tyerman.

found Taylor sorely deficient in evangelical truth. In a letter to his mother he quotes from the *Holy Living* the dictum : ' Whether God has forgiven us or no, we know not : therefore be sorrowful for ever having sinned ' ; and justly observes that ' if we can never have any certainty of our being in a state of salvation . . . we are of all men the most miserable. . . . If we dwell in Christ and Christ in us (which He will not do unless we are regenerate), *certainly we must be sensible of it* '. He was much impressed by William Law's *Christian Perfection* (1726) and *Serious Call* (1729), which he seems to have read as soon as they were published. ' Although I was much offended at many parts of both,' he writes, ' yet they convinced me more than ever of the exceeding height and breadth and depth of the law of God. The light flowed in so mightily upon my soul that everything appeared in a new view. I cried to God for help . . . and by my continued endeavour to keep His whole law, inward and outward, to the utmost of my power, I was persuaded that I should be accepted of God, and that I was even then in a state of salvation.' Many years later he refers again to the same books, and says, looking back on the past, ' These convinced me more than ever of the absolute impossibility of being half a Christian ; and I determined through His grace (the absolute necessity of which I was fully sensible of) to be all-devoted to God, to give Him my soul, my body, and my substance '.[1] Along with his brother Charles he made the acquaintance of Law, and walked from Oxford to visit him on several occasions at the elder Mr. Gibbon's house at Putney. By Law's advice he also read the *Theologia Germanica* and some of the writings of Tauler.

[1] Wesley's *Works*, XI, p. 367.

He received deacon's orders on Sunday, September 19, 1725, and six months later he was elected to a Fellowship at Lincoln College. The latter fact influenced his spiritual history in at least one way. The removal from Christ Church and the change of status made it easier for him to carry out his recent purpose of living a more strict, retired, and religious life. He says in his *Journal*, in May 1738, when recounting his religious experience, ' Removing soon after to another College, I executed a resolution which I was convinced was of the utmost importance – shaking off at once all my trifling acquaintance. I began to see more and more of the value of time. I applied myself closer to study. I watched more carefully against actual sins : I advised others to be religious, according to that scheme of religion by which I modelled my own life '.

After this he was his father's curate for two years in the remote and barbarous hamlet of Wroot, five miles from Epworth. Writing later of his experience here, he says : ' I saw no fruit of my labour. Indeed, it could not be that I should, for I neither laid the foundation of repentance nor of believing the gospel, taking it for granted that all to whom I preached were believers, and that many of them " needed no repentance ".'[1] Meanwhile he had been ordained priest, on September 22, 1728.

During this time Charles Wesley had become serious, and had gathered around him at Oxford a little band of religious associates, the first Methodists. When John returned to Oxford in 1729, he immediately became the leader. Every week they spent ' some evenings together in reading, chiefly the Greek Testament '[2] – a detail which bears upon

[1] Wesley's *Works*, VIII, p. 468.
[2] Wesley's *Works*, VIII, p. 348.

the scholarly knowledge of Scripture that became the basis of Wesley's teaching in after-life. ' In the year 1729', he said long afterwards, 'I began not only to *read* but to *study* the Bible.'[1]   Later, the friends began to visit the sick, and the prisoners in the Castle.   There were four in the little band when it was formed in 1729, and there were only fourteen six years later, when John Wesley left Oxford.

In 1735 he sailed for Oglethorpe's colony of Georgia, with the purpose of becoming a missionary to the Indians.   The voyage was momentous. There were twenty-six Moravians on board the *Simmonds*.   He was impressed by the cheerful faith and the consistent conduct of the Germans ; he learned a good deal from their leaders, especially from Spangenberg in Georgia ; and by his diligent study of their language, begun that he might converse with them, the way was opened for him into all the riches of German hymnology.

His history while in Georgia is complicated by all sorts of troubles, including an unhappy love-affair. His ministry was intensely diligent, devoted, and self-denying, but deplorably bigoted and tactless. All the time, however, his ecclesiastical prejudices were being shaken by the logic of facts.   What his American experience contributed to his spiritual history was really the discipline of a progressive disillusionment.   He was doing the work of the ministry under difficult conditions, in a raw colony seething with the paltriest intrigues, and he was made to feel bitterly the ineffectiveness of his labours. He was also associating with men, in the person of the Moravians, who possessed a far deeper knowledge of the things of God than he did, and he could not but realize the insufficiency of his experience. Wesley tells us of the searching questions Spangen-

[1] Wesley's *Works*, XI, p. 367.

berg asked him the first Sunday that he was in Georgia : ' " Does the Spirit of God bear witness with your spirit that you are a child of God ? " I was surprised, and knew not what to answer. He observed it, and asked, " Do you know Jesus Christ ? " I paused, and said, " I know He is the Saviour of the world." " True," replied he, " but do you know He has saved you ? " I answered, " I hope He has died to save me." He only added, " Do you know yourself ? " I said, " I do." But I fear they were vain words.' On his return to England, Wesley summed up his humbling experiences thus : ' What have I learned myself in the meantime ? Why, (what I the least of all suspected,) that I, who went to America to convert others, was never myself converted to God.' Many years later he modified his judgement : ' I am not sure of this.' But the two and a half years in Georgia did at least reveal to him the utterly unsatisfactory character of his religious attitude and his spiritual experience. It would perhaps not be far from the truth to say of Wesley in these years that he was doing all that he knew for Christ, but that he did not know what Christ had done for him. He was absolutely sincere, and absolutely determined. As far as his will was concerned he was probably as wholly consecrated to the service of God as it was possible for him to be at the time. But he did not yet understand the wonderful privilege of the redeemed soul through trust in Christ. He had not the assurance of pardon, and the vivid sense of Christ's love as a personal possession. Nor did he realize, except in foretastes, the peace that passes understanding, the joy unspeakable, the love that casts out fear. In his own adaptation of the apostolic words, he had the faith of a servant but not the faith of a son.

On his return to England, in February 1738, Wesley wrote : ' If it be said, that I have faith (for many such things have I heard, from many miserable comforters), I answer, So have the devils – a sort of faith ; but still they are strangers to the covenant of promise. So the apostles had even at Cana in Galilee, when Jesus first " manifested forth His glory " ; even then they, in a sort, " believed on Him " ; but they had not then " the faith that overcometh the world ". The faith I want is, " A sure trust and confidence in God, that through the merits of Christ, my sins are forgiven, and I reconciled to the favour of God ". I want that faith which St. Paul recommends to all the world, especially in his Epistle to the Romans : That faith which enables every one that hath it to cry out, " I live not ; but Christ liveth in me ; and the life which I now live, I live by faith in the Son of God, who loved me and gave Himself for me "; *I want that faith which none can have without knowing that he hath it* ; (though many imagine they have it, who have it not ;) for whosoever hath it, is " freed from sin ", the whole " body of sin is destroyed " in him : He is freed from fear, " having peace with God through Christ, and rejoicing in hope of the glory of God ". And he is freed from doubt, " having the love of God shed abroad in his heart, through the Holy Ghost which is given unto him ", which " Spirit itself beareth witness with his spirit, that he is a child of God ".'

We now seek to trace how he attained the assurance of faith. Six days after he landed in England, on his return from Georgia, he met Peter Böhler. It was on Tuesday, February 7, 1738, ' a day much to be remembered', as he remarks in his *Journal*. Böhler was a native of Frankfort-on-Main, and was educated at the Universities of Jena and Leipzig.

He had been brought to God amid Pietist influences
as a student, and had then come under the spell of
Count Zinzendorf. In the previous December he
had been ordained a minister of the Church of
the United Brethren by Zinzendorf and Nitsch-
mann, in the Chapel of the Ronneburg. He had
then been commissioned to go to Georgia as pastor
of the Moravian congregation at Savannah, and
missionary to the natives of that region. He was
now on his way to America. Wesley seems to have
been attracted to him at once. They saw a good
deal of each other during the next three months in
London and at Oxford. Böhler's contribution to
Wesley's experience consisted in his positive teaching as to assurance, and as to its being often bestowed
in a moment. On Sunday, April 23, Böhler drove
Wesley out of his last hesitancy as to the possibility
and the fact by the personal testimony of some
recent converts. ' I was beat out of this retreat,
too, by the concurring evidence of several living
witnesses, who testify God had thus wrought in
themselves, giving them in a moment such a faith
in the blood of His Son as translated them out of
darkness into light, out of sin and fear into holiness
and happiness. Here ended my disputing. I could
now only cry out, " Lord, help Thou mine un-
belief ! " ' Böhler's account of this is fuller, and he
tells us that when Wesley was convinced by these
testimonies, he said, ' We will sing that hymn,
" Hier legt mein Sinn sich vor dir nieder " (My
soul before Thee prostrate lies), during the singing
of which he often wiped his eyes '. The words must
have expressed exactly Wesley's spiritual attitude :

> Lost and undone, for aid I cry ;
> In Thy death, Saviour, let me die !
> Grieved with Thy grief, pained with Thy pain,
> Ne'er may I feel self-love again.

When my warmed thoughts I fix on Thee,
And plunge me in Thy Mercy's sea,
Then even on me Thy face shall shine,
And quicken this dead heart of mine !¹

Böhler left London on May 4, and on the 13th
Wesley was 'a little refreshed' by a Latin letter
from him, written when the ship was off Southamp-
ton, in which he prays that Wesley 'may taste, and
then see, how exceedingly the Son of God has loved
you, and loves you still ; and that so you may continually trust in Him, and feel His life in yourself'.

Within a fortnight of this fell the most critical
day of Wesley's life.   During the interval, as he
himself remarks, his experience was marked by two
new notes – an absolute renunciation of 'all dependence, in whole or in part, upon my own works
of righteousness, on which I had really grounded
my hope of salvation, though I knew it not, from
my youth up' ; and 'continual prayer for this very
thing – justifying, saving faith, a full reliance on
the blood of Christ shed for me ; a trust in Him as
my Christ, as my sole justification, sanctification,
and redemption'.

The religious experience of Charles Wesley had
been roughly parallel to that of his brother.   He
had been at Westminster School, where his brother
Samuel was Usher.   Thence he had been elected to a
Studentship at Christ Church.   He went to Oxford
determined to enjoy himself, and seems to have
wasted most of his first year in diversions. His
brother John says, ' If I spoke to him about religion,
he would warmly answer, " What, would you have
me to be a saint all at once ? " and would hear no
more '.   It was while John was at Wroot that

¹ This hymn is by C. F. Richter, the physician of the Waisenhaus at Halle.
It appeared first in Freylinghausen's *Gesangbuch* in 1704.   Wesley trans-
lated it while he was in Georgia in 1736, as appears from an entry in his
Diary at the end of November in that year.

Charles began to think seriously about religion. He says, ' Diligence led me into serious thinking. I went to the weekly Sacrament, and persuaded two or three young students to accompany me, and to observe the method of study prescribed by the statutes of the University. This gained me the harmless name of *Methodist* '. Such was the origin of a name borne to-day by millions of Christian people ! When John Wesley returned to Oxford in 1729 he found a little company of students associated with his brother, and known by this name of ' Methodists ', and, as we have seen, he speedily became their leader.

Charles Wesley accompanied his brother to Georgia, having been recently ordained. He had a troubled time in America, and returned before his brother. He met Böhler in Oxford, and a little later the German visited him, when he was very ill, in Westminster. Böhler asked him what hope of salvation he had, and why, and he replied, ' Because I have used my best endeavours to serve God '. Böhler said nothing, but shook his head. Charles Wesley saw what the Moravian meant, and thought him unkind, but he could not help asking himself afterward whether it was sufficient to stake his soul's hope on his own efforts and his own sincerity. After this he sought diligently for the simplicity of faith and the assurance of salvation.

The great experience came to Charles Wesley before it came to his brother. William Holland, one of the Moravians, wrote at the time, ' Being providentially directed to Martin Luther's *Commentary on the Epistle to the Galatians*, I carried it round to Mr. Charles Wesley, who was then sick at Mr. Bray's '. Charles Wesley himself wrote in his *Journal* under the date of May 17, 1738, ' Today I first saw Luther on the Galatians, which Mr.

Holland had accidentally lit upon. We began, and found him nobly full of faith '. Later in the day he wrote, ' I spent some hours this evening in private with Martin Luther, who was greatly blessed to me, especially his conclusion of the second chapter. I laboured, waited, and prayed to feel, " Who loved *me*, and gave Himself for *me* " '. Three days afterward, on Sunday, May 21, he found that great assurance of the love of Christ.

It is easy enough to identify the precise passage in Luther's great exposition that counted for so much in Charles Wesley's experience, because he mentions ' the conclusion of the second chapter ', and quotes the Apostle's words, ' Who loved me, and gave Himself for me '. There was an English version of Luther's *Commentary on the Galatians* by an unnamed translator, first issued in 1575, with an Address to the Reader signed *Edwinus London*, (i.e. Edwin Sandys, the Bishop of London, who became Archbishop of York the following year, and died in 1588). This translation was re-issued, by the way, in 1760, with a commendatory Preface by Martin Madan. This sixteenth-century English version renders Luther's comment on the last words of the second chapter of the Epistle thus : ' Read therefore with great vehemency these words, *me* and *for me*, and so inwardly practise with thyself, that thou, with a sure faith, mayst conceive and print this *me* in thy heart, and apply it unto thyself, not doubting but thou art of the number of those to whom this *me* belongeth : also that Christ hath not only loved Peter and Paul and given Himself for them, but that the same grace also which is comprehended in this *me*, as well pertaineth and cometh unto us, as unto them. For as we cannot deny but that we are all sinners, and are constrained to say that through the sin of Adam we are all lost, were made the enemies of God, subject to the wrath and judgement of God, and guilty of eternal death (for this do all terrified hearts feel and confess, and more indeed than they should do :) so can we not deny but that Christ died for our sins, that he might make us righteous. For he died not to justify the righteous, but the unrighteous, and to make them the children of God, and inheritors of all spiritual and heavenly gifts. Therefore, when I feel and confess myself to be a sinner through Adam's transgression, why should I not say, that I am made righteous through the righteousness of Christ, especially when I hear that he loved *me*, and gave himself *for me* ? This did Paul most stedfastly believe, and therefore he speaketh these words with so great vehemency and full assurance.'

The Latin text of the passage (we shall see later that it may very probably have been read in Latin) is as follows : ' Lege igitur cum magna emphasi has voces : '' ME, PRO ME '', et assuefacias te, ut illud, '' ME '' possis certa fide concipere et applicare tibi, Neque dubites, quin etiam sis ex numero eorum, qui dicuntur (ME). Item, quod Christus non tantum dilexerit Petrum et Paulum et seipsum pro eis tradiderit, sed quod illa gratia aeque ad nos pertineat et veniat ac ad illos, Ideo etiam comprehendimur in isto '' ME ''. Sicut enim negare non possumus nos omnes esse peccatores, et cogimur dicere Adam peccato suo perdidisse nos, fecisse nos hostes Dei, obnoxios irae et iudicio Dei et reos aeternae mortis (hoc enim sentiunt et fatentur territa corda, et plus aequo), Ita negare non possumus, quin Christus pro peccatis nostris mortuus sit, ut iustificaremur. Non enim mortuus est, ut iustos faceret iustos, sed ut peccatores faceret iustos, amicos et filios Dei et heredes omnium bonorum coelestium. Cum igitur me peccatorem sentio et fateor propter transgressionem Adae, cur non dicerem me iustum propter iustitiam Christi, praesertim cum audiam eum dilexisse me, et tradidisse seipsum pro me ? Paulus hoc firmissime credidit, ideo etiam cum tanta plerophoria loqui-tur.'[1]

Luther's loving emphasis on St. Paul's words is remembered and recalled in some of the hymns written at the time :

> And can it be that *I* should gain
>   An interest in the Saviour's blood ?
> Died He *for me*, who caused His pain ?
>   *For me*, who Him to death pursued ?
> Amazing love ! how can it be
> That Thou, my God, shouldst die *for me* !

And throughout a long hymn written a year later, and entitled ' For the Anniversary Day of One's Conversion ' :

> Then with my *heart* I first believed,
>   Believed with faith divine ;
> Power with the Holy Ghost received
>   To call the Saviour *mine*.
> I felt my Lord's atoning blood
>   Close to *my* soul applied ;
> *Me, me*, He loved – the Son of God
>   *For me, for me*, He died !

Three days after his brother had found the peace of God, a like experience came to John Wesley. It was on Wednesday, May 24, 1738. He has left us a minute record of the day. In the morning he was comforted by a word of Scripture, ' There are given unto us exceeding great and precious promises, even that ye should be partakers of the divine nature ', and later in the day by another : ' Thou

[1] Luther, *In epistolam S. Pauli ad Galatas Commentarius* (*Werke*, XL, pp. 299–300).

art not far from the kingdom of God.' In the afternoon he was asked to go to St. Paul's, and the words of the anthem helped him : ' O Israel, trust in the Lord ; for with the Lord there is mercy, and with Him is plenteous redemption. And He shall redeem Israel from all his sins.' But the great experience came at night. ' In the evening I went very unwillingly to a Society in Aldersgate Street, where one was reading Luther's *Preface to the Epistle to the Romans*. About a quarter before nine, while he was describing the change which God works in the heart through faith in Christ, I felt my heart strangely warmed. I felt I did trust in Christ, in Christ alone, for salvation. And an assurance was given me that He had taken away my sins, even mine, and saved me from the law of sin and death.'

Can we identify the very passage in Luther's *Preface to the Epistle to the Romans* that brought light to John Wesley's soul ? It is easy to be sure of the words that meant so much to Charles Wesley, as we have seen, because of his allusion to the precise passage in the Epistle to the Galatians. We have no such explicit guidance with respect to the momentous words in the *Preface to the Epistle to the Romans*. I think that nevertheless we may be quite sure of the very words. There is one passage, and perhaps only one, that answers in every respect to the requirements of the hour.

The passage reads, in the Latin text : ' Legem autem implere, est facere ea, quae lex mandat corde hilari et erecto et alacri, id, est sponte et ultro Deo vivere et bene operari, etiam si nulla esset lex. Talis vero alacritas, hilaritas, et propensa voluntas ac ardens affectus non contingit cordibus, nisi per spiritum vivificatorem, et vivum eius impulsum ac agitationem in corde, sicut capitulo quinto dicit.

Spiritus vero donatur per solam fidem in Iesum Christum, quaemadmodum initio dixit Apostolus. Fides est per auditum Evangelii seu verbi Dei, per quod praedicatur Christus pro nobis mortuus, sepultus et suscitatus a mortuis, ut Cap. III, IV et X dicit. Tota igitur iustificatio ex Deo est, fides et spiritus ex Deo sunt et non ex nobis. Hinc et sola fides iustificat, solaque legem implet. Fides enim per meritum Christi impetrat spiritum sanctum. Hic spiritus cor novat, exhilarat, et excitat et inflammat, ut sponte faciat ea, quae vult lex. Ac tum demum ex fide sic in corde efficaciter agente et vivente, sponte fluunt opera vere bona. Hoc vult Capite III. Nam cum ibi damnasset prorsus opera legis, et potuisset videri legem, per fidei doctrinam destructurus et aboliturus, per occupationem occurrit, Legem (inquit) non destruimus, sed stabilimus. Id est docemus quomodo lex credendo seu per fidem, vere impleatur.'[1]

The corresponding passage in Luther's German reads : ' Aber das Gesetz erfüllen ist, mit lust und liebe seine werck thun, und frey on des Gesetzes zwang göttlich und wol leben, als were kein Gesetze oder straffe. Solche lust aber freier liebe, gibt der heilige Geist ins hertz, wie er spricht im V Capit. Der Geist aber wird nicht denn allein, in, mit und durch den glauben an Jhesum Christ, gegeben, wie er in der Vorrede saget. So kompt der glaube nicht, on alleine durch Gottes wort oder Euangelium, das Christum prediget, wie er ist Gottes Son und Mensch, gestorben und aufferstanden umb unsern willen, Wie er am III. IV. und X. Cap. saget. Daher kompts, das allein der Glaube gerecht machet, und das Gesetz erfüllet, Denn er bringet den Geist aus Christus verdienst. Der Geist aber machet ein lüstig und frey hertz, wie

---

[1] Luther, *Praefatio in Epistolam Pauli ad Romanos* (*Werke*, V, p. 621).

das Gesetz foddert, so gehen denn die guten werck
aus dem glauben selber. Das meinet er am III.
Cap. nach dem er des Gesetzes werck verworffen
hatte, das es lautet, als wolt er das Gesetz auffheben
durch den Glauben, Nein (spricht er) wir richten
das Gesetz an, durch den Glauben, das ist, wir
erfüllens durch den glauben.'[1]

There was at least one seventeenth-century
English translation of Luther's *Preface to the Epistle
to the Romans*. It is entitled ' *A Methodicall Preface
prefixed before the Epistle of S. Paul to the Romans, verie
necessarie and profitable for the better understanding of it,
Made by the right reverend Father and faithfull servant of
Christ Iesus, Martin Luther*, now newly translated out
of Latin into English, by W. W., Student '. The
date of the volume is 1632. It renders the passage
in question thus : ' To fulfil the Law is to do those
things which the Law commandeth with a cheerful
and willing heart ; that is, freely and of thine own
accord to live unto God, and to work well, though
there were no Law at all. Such a cheerfulness,
readiness, willingness, and ardent affection, cannot
come into our hearts but by the quickening Spirit,
and His lively impulsions and agitations in our
heart. Now the Spirit is given only by faith in
Christ. Faith cometh through the hearing of the
Gospel, through which word Christ is preached to
us, to have died, to have been buried, and to have
risen again from death for us. Therefore our whole
justification is of God. Faith also and the Spirit
are of God : they come not of ourselves. Where-
fore let us conclude that faith alone justifies, and
that faith alone fulfilleth the Law. For faith
through the merit of Christ obtaineth the Holy
Spirit, which Spirit doth make us new hearts, doth
exhilarate us, doth excite and inflame our heart,

[1] Luther, *Vorrede auf die Epistel S. Pauli an die Römer* (*Werke*, VII, p. 7).

that it may do those things willingly, of love, which the Law commandeth ; and so, at the last, good works indeed do proceed freely from the faith which worketh so mightily, and which is so lively in our hearts. This is the meaning of the third Chapter. For whereas he had utterly damned the works of the Law, and might have seemed to have disannulled and abolished the Law by the teaching the doctrine of faith, he preventeth that objection in these words. We do not (saith he) destroy the Law, but rather establish it. That is, we teach how the Law may be truly fulfilled by faith, that is, by believing in Christ Jesus.'

It is possible that the passage was read in the English of this or some other translation. But it is far more likely that it was read in the Latin, or in Luther's own German. We know that Molther sometimes addressed the Society at Fetter Lane in Latin and sometimes in German. When he spoke in Latin, James Hutton (who first introduced him to the Society) acted as his interpreter, and when he spoke in German it was Richard Viney (who was in Germany at the same time as Wesley, and who apparently knew German better than Wesley did) who served in that capacity. Viney also interpreted for Peter Böhler when he spoke in German. Wesley himself, of course, would need no translation from either language. I am strongly inclined to believe, on the whole, that the passage was read in Latin. It is perhaps more likely that some one would have a copy of the Latin than that any member of the Society would possess an English version that was more than a hundred years old at the time, and there does not seem to have been a more recent translation. But it is possible that the passage was read in German, for one of the Germans might easily enough have possessed a copy of

Luther's own words in his own tongue. Whatever was the language, there can be little doubt that this was the passage. The evangelical sentiment conveyed in these sentences is precisely the kind of truth that Wesley needed at the time, to show him the way to an assurance of pardon and peace, and there is a rather striking verbal parallel between Wesley's own words, ' I felt my heart strangely warmed . . .' and the phrase, ' Hic spiritus cor novat, exhilarat, et excitat et inflammat '. It is a striking fact, and surely also a symbolical one, that both the Wesleys were led into a really evangelical experience of religion by words of St. Paul, interpreted and emphasized by Luther. As Coleridge said, with real insight, ' the only fit commentator on St. Paul was Luther – not by any means such a gentleman, but almost as great a genius '.

Luther used to say that there was a great deal of religion in the prepositions. The whole secret of Wesley's experience on this memorable day may be said to lie in the pronouns. ' An assurance was given *me* that *He* had taken away *my* sins, even *mine*, and saved *me*.' *He* . . . *mine* . . . *me* . . . *!* The momentous fact in Wesley's experience at this time was a new, sudden, vivid, personal *realization* of what he had always believed. He had been taught from childhood that Christ loved us, and died for us, the righteous for the unrighteous, to bring us to God. All his life long he had believed that, in the very imperfect sense of accepting it as a part of the Christian creed. Latterly he had striven to believe it more simply, and more passionately. But now he realized it for himself. That which had long been a part of his creed and of his thought suddenly became a personal experience. He knew for himself, in an intensely and intimately personal way, the redeeming love of the Lord Jesus Christ. In

this essential matter the experience of the two
brothers is exactly parallel, as we should expect.
What they had both believed, as they thought, from
their childhood, they now realized for themselves,
in the experience which each at the time called his
conversion.   Faith, in the New Testament sense, is
not an act of assent, or even an act of credence, but
a personal trust in Christ, and what came to John
Wesley in the hour when his heart was strangely
warmed, was a personal faith in a personal Saviour,
an intimate assurance in his own soul of the redeeming mercy of Christ.

Henceforth Wesley's life was on another level.
There were fluctuations of feeling, naturally, but
what he gained that day he never lost.   His life was
changed.   He had a new peace.   ' My soul continued in peace, but yet in heaviness because of
manifold temptations. . . . I waked in peace, but
not in joy. . . . I have constant peace. . . . I had still
more comfort, and peace, and joy.' Wesley's
equable temperament did not lend itself to great
transports of joy, but henceforth the peace of God
was his.   It was the peace of spiritual victory.   He
had power over sin.   ' Herein I found the difference between this and my former state chiefly consisted.   I was striving – yea, fighting – with all my
might under the law, as well as under grace.   But
then I was sometimes, if not often, conquered ;
now, I was always conqueror.'[1]   It was the peace
of utter trust.   He had greatly feared death, and
with characteristic honesty had recognized that
fear as a proof of the unsatisfactory nature of his
religious experience.   ' Whoever is uneasy on any
account (bodily pain alone excepted) carries in
himself his own conviction that he is so far an un-
believer.   Is he uneasy at the apprehension of

[1] See the *Journal*, under the dates May 24, 25, 28, June 6, 1738.

death ? Then he believeth not that " to die is
gain "... I can talk well – nay, and believe myself,
while no danger is near. But let death look me in
the face, and my spirit is troubled.'[1] So he had
written on the voyage home. But now he was rid
of that ' sin of fear ', to use the phrase of Donne that
he often quoted. He never feared death again in
any of the perils or sicknesses of his life, from the
day that he ' felt his heart strangely warmed ' to the
day, more than fifty years later, when he died with
the words of triumph on his lips, ' The best of all is,
God is with us ! '   And there had come to him also
a spiritual energy, an evangelical zeal, an unction
of the Holy One, that he had never before possessed.
That hour in Aldersgate Street was the real beginning of his unique apostolate. He recognized this
himself. Writing in 1746, he remarked that from
1725 to 1729 he ' preached much ', but ' saw no
fruit of his labour ' – naturally, since he did not
preach either repentance or faith ; that from 1729
to 1734, ' laying a deeper foundation of repentance ',
he ' saw a little fruit ' ; that from 1734 to 1738,
' speaking more of faith in Christ ', he ' saw more
fruit ' ; but that ' from 1738 to this time, speaking
continually of Jesus Christ . . . making Him all in
all . . . the Word of God ran as fire among the
stubble ; it was glorified more and more ; multitudes crying out, " What must we do to be saved ? "
and afterward witnessing, " By grace we are saved
through faith ".'[2]

It is almost impossible to overestimate the importance of what happened to John Wesley on May
24, 1738. Lecky said that the hour of Wesley's conversion was ' an epoch in English history ', and the
phrase is not an exaggeration. But a determined

---

[1] See the *Journal*, under the dates December 28, 1737, and January 24, 1738.
[2] Wesley's *Works*, VIII, p. 468.

attempt has been made by more than one writer
to minimize the importance of the experience.
Dr. Maximin Piette has declared that 1725, when
he was preparing for his ordination, was the date of
Wesley's *première et vraie conversion*,[1] and, many years
before Dr. Piette, another French writer, Dr.
Augustin Leger, had similarly argued that Wesley's
conversion, in the sense that his soul then first definitely turned to God, should be dated in 1725,
and not in 1738, and that *qualifier celle-ci de ' conversion evangélique ' prête encore à une confusion de mots
qui aboutit fatalement à une confusion de choses, à de
profondes méprises et à de graves mécomptes*.[2] There
is surely a real confusion here, both of words and of
realities, but it does not lie where Dr. Leger thought.
No one doubts that there was a real experience in
1725 ; no one disputes that it may be regarded as
the proper beginning of Wesley's religious life, in so
far as any such thing can be dated at all. But the
unique importance of what happened on May 24,
1738, stands out for all to see, because of its results
in Wesley's life and work. If it had not happened,
there would have been no Evangelical Revival, as
far as one can tell. John Wesley might have lived a
religious life, rather ascetic and rather melancholy ;
he might have written some religious books, full of
meticulous rules of piety and formal devotions ;
he might have fulfilled a useful and blameless career
as a Fellow of his college, or as a country parson ;
but he would never have possessed the deep experience of assurance and peace and joy, and he would
never have re-created religion in England as he did.

[1] A partir de sa première et vraie conversion, en 1725, quand John
s'est appliqué à la vie intérieure, à la lecture de l'*Imitation* et des auteurs
ascétiques, se préparant ainsi à l'ordination sacerdotale, la préoccupation
dominante de son âme fut son propre progrès dans la vie spirituelle. – *La
Réaction Wesléyenne dans l'Évolution Protestante*, p. 577.

[2] *La Jeunesse de Wesley*, p. 366.

The world would never have heard of Wesley, and that *conquête religieuse de l'Angleterre par un Christianisme renouvelé* of which Dr. Leger himself speaks would never have come to pass.

There is something artificial in these contentions, after all. Does any one think for a moment that the Wesley of 1725, even if he had been older at the time, could have done the work that the Wesley of 1738 did ? No one could imagine such a thing. Whatever you call the experience of 1738, then, it was that which made Wesley the man he was and enabled him to do the work he did. It really does not matter whether you call it his conversion or not. On any and every possible interpretation of it, it was a spiritual event that gave Wesley quite a new sort of religious experience, with an assurance and a power and a peace and a joy he had never known before, and it was this change that made him into the Apostle of England. Apart from it he might have been an eighteenth-century clergyman of the best type, with a perfectly sincere religion of a rather formal, ecclesiastical, and intolerant kind, but he would never have been the man who led the Evangelical Revival. Surely that is as plain as anything can well be.

At that point it really becomes a dispute about nomenclature. For if it be admitted (and I do not see how any one can possibly deny it) that what happened in Aldersgate Street on the night of May 24, 1738, was the transforming experience of Wesley's life, without which he would not have been the man he was, and would not have done the work he did, for more than fifty years afterward – then it does not matter whether you call it his conversion, or his evangelical conversion, or what else you like. It was in any case the one, great, definite, critical experience of his religious life.

It is true that at first Wesley used some unguarded expressions as to his new experience, speaking as if he had never been a Christian in any real sense until now, and as if no one could be a Christian without such an experience of assurance. But all this was very natural. When any great experience comes to us for the first time we are apt to think that it is the most vital and most revolutionary thing that ever happened, and to wonder that other men do not seem to realize this. That is merely human nature. In later life Wesley frankly confessed that he was wrong in his early insistence upon two things – the necessity and the suddenness of the experience – and admitted both that it was not possessed by some who were real Christians, though it was the privilege of all, and also that the experience might come gradually. He said, in 1745, in a letter to ' Mr. John Smith ', the pseudonym of Dr. Secker, the Bishop of Oxford, ' I do not deny that God imperceptibly works in some a gradually increasing assurance of His love ; but I am equally certain He works in others a full assurance thereof in one moment '. According to Southey's account, Wesley said in his old age to Melville Horne, ' When fifty years ago my brother Charles and I, in the simplicity of our hearts, told the good people of England that unless they *knew* their sins forgiven they were under the wrath and curse of God, I marvel, Melville, they did not stone us ! The Methodists, I hope, know better now : we preach assurance as we always did, as a common privilege of the children of God ; but we do not enforce it, under the pain of damnation, denounced on all who enjoy it not '.

This must not be misunderstood. Wesley never ceased to proclaim that it was the privilege of every believer to know his sins forgiven, and that this was the most vital fact in the experience of religion. But he came to see that there were many sincere followers of Christ who did not possess this great assurance, either because it had been doubted or denied as a normal privilege of the believing soul, or because it had been obscured by a superstitious stress upon the rites of the Church, as if the only assurance that a believer could have depended upon a priestly absolution. But Wesley and his followers have always maintained that every penitent and believing soul may possess, and ought to possess, an assurance of salvation.

Any study of the religious experience of Wesley would be incomplete without some stress upon another aspect of it. If there ever was a man in this world who deserved to be venerated as a saint, Wesley was one, and yet he has not been generally regarded in that light. Doubtless this is because the general conception of saintliness has not yet recovered from the influence of monasticism, with its ascetic tradition, and its doctrine of the opposition between the active and the contemplative life. The saintly life was associated in the popular mind for many centuries with retirement from the world, and an existence almost wholly passed in meditation and mortification. The very activity of Wesley in the service of God has hindered our recognition of his holiness. Fletcher, with his life of comparative quietude, has become the typical saint of early Methodism. And yet if there is to be a comparison between the two men, as Dr. Adam Clarke once said, it was Wesley who must have had the deeper intimacy with God in the midst of his amazing labours.

His habits of devotion are very significant. In his life of unexampled activity he always spent a full hour in solitary devotion at the beginning of the day. Besides this, he passed many hours of almost every day, while on his journeys, in reading and meditation, ' as much alone as if in a wilderness ', as he said himself. Then his knowledge of the Scriptures (especially of the Greek Testament) was such as could only have resulted from patient, loving, lifelong study. It is significant also that the spiritual fellowship of his own people seems to have been a great factor in his religious life. ' I need heat more than light,' he said to Henry Moore, and therefore, as Moore adds, he delighted especially in the devotional meetings of the Societies. These last words of Wesley's mark the type of his saintliness. His temperament was calm, and he was much dominated by his intellect, which was severely logical. Accordingly his spiritual experience does not seem to have been very emotional or ecstatic. But it was characterized by a quiet, thankful, and satisfying sense of the favour of God. The chief notes of Wesley's saintliness may be said to be utter consecration and absolute trust. He laid out his life, in the most deliberate way, for the glory of God. He withheld nothing. His gifts, his time, his reputation, his ease – all were surrendered, and, if there were need, sacrificed to the work of God. It is impossible to exaggerate the completeness of Wesley's dedication of himself, and all that he had, to this high service. And he had an invulnerable trust in God. He was charged with anxious responsibilities that would have reduced most men to fretful despair. But he never worried. ' I feel and I grieve,' he said, ' but by the grace of God I fret at nothing.' He declared that he had never lost a quarter of an hour's sleep through worrying over his many anxieties. This was not merely due to an equable temperament : it was much more the result of a sure faith. Hence his religion was cheerful : he said that ' sour godliness is the devil's

religion'.   Surely there is not, in the whole calendar
of saints, any man who ever devoted himself more
absolutely to the service of Christ, whose soul lived
more constantly in communion with God, or whose
whole conduct, in word and deed, showed more
fully the spirit expressed in his brother's lines :

> So may the fervour of my zeal
> Be the pure flame of love !

Chapter II

METHODISM AND THE PAST

METHODISM is the most modern of the great evangelical movements which have appeared from age to age in the history of the Church. But it has many interesting links with the past. It is one of the most impressive lessons of history that nothing ever appears in this world that is absolutely new. The fresh flame is always kindled from the ancient fires. The Renaissance started from the re-discovery of the language and the culture of Greece. The Reformation began with a return to the New Testament and primitive Christianity. It is always so, and in religion especially every new movement is really a revival, in the proper sense of the word – a renewal of the faith and the experience of the earliest age.

It is interesting to note the numerous strands which connect Methodism in the eighteenth century with movements and tendencies in the life of the Church in past times, both before and after the Reformation. Methodism was definitely indebted to the Reformers, to Pietism, to Moravianism, and to mysticism, and all these connexions and cross-connexions carry us far back into the history of the Church in earlier days. Thus Methodism owed much to Moravianism, and Moravianism in turn owed much to Pietism. Both movements, again, went back to the Reformers, and both were indebted to the medieval mystics, and the evangelical sects which existed before the Reformers. Wesley and the early Methodists, again, were directly influenced at some points by Pietism ; and also by the mystics, whom they came to know through Law, through the Moravians, and through the Pietists. The eighteenth-century Moravianism that Wesley knew had links, again, with the Bohemian Brethren, and the obscure evangelical movements which dated from before the Reformation. All these strands are entangled in a most intricate way.

Thus it is a striking fact, as we have seen, that both the Wesleys were led into the evangelical experience of religion by some of Luther's words ; in the one instance, a passage in the *Preface to the Epistle to the Romans*, in the other, a passage in the *Commentary on the Epistle to the Galatians*, and in both cases Luther's phrases were comments upon either some characteristic thought, or some express word, of the Apostle Paul. This is surely neither accidental nor insignificant. Early Methodism recovered the spirit of the Reformation as the Reformation recovered the spirit of the New Testament. Each was a return to the reality of spiritual and experimental religion after a period when religion had degenerated into mere ceremonialism or mere moralism. Then it is noteworthy that the words of Luther were brought to the notice of both the Wesleys through the Moravians, and that does not by any means exhaust the debt of Methodism to the Church of the Brethren.

Methodism owed much, directly and indirectly, to Pietism. Pietism is the one religious movement that most closely resembles Methodism. It revived religion in Germany, in the seventeenth century, in a way that singularly resembles the Evangelical Revival in this land in some of its details, and it has points, not only of resemblance, but of actual connexion with Methodism.[1] Pietism began with the work of Philip Jakob Spener, who was born in 1635 and died in 1705. He was educated at the University of Strassburg, and then went to Basle, where he was a pupil of the younger Buxtorf, the most famous Hebraist of the day, and thence to Geneva, where he was influenced by Labadie, the mystic, whose *Manuel de Prière* he translated into German. After this he became pastor at Strassburg, where he also lectured at the University on philosophy and history. But the real work of his life began when he became pastor at Frankfort in 1666. He found the spiritual life of the Church there at a very low ebb, but his evangelical preaching and a vigorous revival of catechetical instruction soon began to make a change for the better. In 1670 he gathered some of the more earnest folk of the Church into a group, which met in his study to read devotional books, discuss the subject of the last sermon, and generally promote the spiritual life of the members. Then meetings of a like kind began to be held in other houses, and in 1682 Spener obtained permission for the gatherings to be held in the church. These were the famous *collegia pietatis*. In 1675 Spener published his *Pia Desideria*, in which he gave an account of his aims and methods. He pleaded for more simple and more evangelical preaching, for family worship, for closer study of the Bible in these groups of earnest believers – *ecclesiolae in ecclesia* – and generally for a revival of spiritual life. The influence of Spener himself, and of the groups that he inaugurated, led to a real

[1] Der Methodismus hat freilich mancherlei mit dem deutschen Pietismus des endenden 17 und der ersten Hälfte des 18 Jahrhunderts gemein ; ja er ist vorbereitet durch die Anfänge einer Erweckung in England, die mit dem Spener-Franckeschen Pietismus genetisch zusammenhängt, und Herrnhuter Einflüsse haben bei seinem selbstständigen Hervortreten ein entscheidende Rolle gespielt, einzelne seiner Einrichtungen dauernd beeinflusst. – Loofs, 'Methodismus', in Herzog-Hauck *Encyklopädie*, Heft 119, p. 750.

revival of experimental religion in the Church in Germany.

Now Spener was much influenced in his early days by the writings of Johann Arndt, especially the books entitled *Vom wahren Christenthum* and *Paradies-gärtlein*, which were also extremely popular among the Pietists generally in later days.[1] Arndt was a forerunner of Pietism, for the work of his life was the promotion of experimental religion. He was deeply influenced by Tauler and other mystics. It is noteworthy that Spener himself not only studied, but published editions of, the *Theologia Germanica* and of Tauler's *Sermons*. There was another edition of the latter book for the use of Pietists issued later by the press of the Orphan House at Halle, along with other mystical books, including a German translation of some of Poiret's writings. It is interesting to note that from the same source there also issued an edition of the *Historia Fratrum Bohemorum* of Comenius.

Spener was also influenced in early life by some English books of the Puritan school, in particular some of the writings of Baxter, which seem to have been read a good deal in Germany, especially along the Rhine, at that period. This is a very interesting detail, for here we have the Puritanism of England helping to promote Pietism in Germany, and then Pietism in turn definitely influences Methodism in England. There cannot be much doubt that it was the reading of Baxter's *Gildas Salvianus, the Reformed Pastor*, that was largely the inspiration of Spener's methods. The diligent study of the Bible, more effective methods of catechetical instruction, the discussion of the experimental aspects of religion,

---

[1] It may be noted that Arvid Gradin, one of the Moravians at Herrnhut whose religious experience Wesley carefully records, owed his spiritual awakening to the reading of Arndt's book *Vom wahren Christenthum*.

and more intimate fellowship in the spiritual life, were the very things for which Baxter pleaded, and the very things which the *collegia pietatis* promoted.

Spener was succeeded in the leadership of the movement by August Hermann Francke, who was born at Lübeck in 1663. He studied at Leipzig, and met Spener in 1688. He lectured at Leipzig to crowded assemblies of students on the Epistles of St. Paul, until the lectures were forbidden by the theological faculty. Then he was called to Erfurt as pastor, and his earnest preaching filled the church, but after a time he was suddenly banished from the place. A new university was being founded at Halle, and in 1691 Francke was appointed Professor of Oriental Languages there, and later Professor of Theology. At Halle, Francke carried on the movement, and gave it a new direction in the way of social, charitable, and educational work. In 1695 he took an orphan child into his home ; before the next year began he had a dozen. The number kept on increasing, and in 1698 the famous Waisenhaus was built. There was also a charity school, which had two thousand scholars. A dispensary and a printing establishment for the production of religious books were presently added, and the Franckeschen Stiftungen at Halle are still amongst the greatest institutions of the kind in Europe. Francke wrote an account of the origin and development of all this work at Halle in the *Pietas Hallensis*.

Francke died in 1727, and was succeeded by Johann Anastasius Freylinghausen, his son-in-law. He is memorable for the *Gesangbuch* which he issued in 1704. It became the hymnal of the Pietists. Wesley possessed a copy (though he only used it as the tune-book to accompany the Herrnhut

Gesangbuch), and he translated many hymns by Pietists which the Moravians had inserted in their collection—two by Freylinghausen ; two by Christian Friedrich Richter, who was the physician of the Waisenhaus ; one by Joachim Lange, who was Professor of Divinity at Halle ; one by Gottfried Arnold, the ecclesiastical historian, who was a disciple of Spener ; and two by Gerhard Tersteegen, who was also connected with Pietism. Moreover, Bengel, who was the greatest expositor of the age, and the real founder of the criticism of the New Testament text in Germany, as Dorner called him, was a product of Pietism, and it was his *Gnomon of the New Testament* that Wesley chose, with scholarly instinct, as the basis of his own *Notes on the New Testament*. There were several other ways in which Pietism influenced Wesley. He records in his *Diary* that he began to read the *Pietas Hallensis* on November 6, 1735, and another book of Francke's, *Nicodemus, or a Treatise on the Fear of Man*, on November 18 of the same year. He published an abridged translation of the latter in 1740. When Wesley was at Halle in July 1738 he wished to visit Francke's son, but found that he was out of town. Wesley did succeed in meeting him a little later, on August 19. On the same visit he inspected with interest the great institutions which Francke had founded. Wesley intended the Orphan House at Newcastle, which was one of the earliest Methodist buildings, to be on the lines of the Waisenhaus at Halle, though the design was never really fulfilled.

Then Methodism is distinctly linked up with the Religious Societies which existed in the late seventeenth and the early eighteenth centuries, and these again, as we shall see, are connected with Pietism. The Religious Societies were established in the seventeenth century by Dr. Smithies, the Rector of St. Giles, Cripplegate ; Dr. Beveridge, the Rector of St. Peter's, Cornhill; and Dr. Horneck, who was the Lutheran minister at the Savoy Church. Now Dr. Horneck, who was certainly the principal promoter of these Societies, was a Pietist, and there can be no doubt that they were at least partly suggested by the *collegia pietatis* which were so characteristic of the movements in Germany.

Anthony Horneck was a native of Bacharach on the Rhine, where he was born in the year 1641. He was a student at Heidelberg, and then at Oxford. He came to England about 1661. He became preacher at the Savoy in 1671, and was extremely popular, drawing people from all over London to his services. Evelyn the diarist says that he was ' a most pathetic preacher and a person of saint-like life '. It was through the preaching of Horneck, and the other zealous clergymen who have been mentioned, about the year 1670 and onwards, that many people were awakened to the life of religion, and it was upon their advice that these folk began to meet together for mutual edification. Those who had been aroused in spirit were ' counselled to meet together once a week, and to apply themselves to good discourse, and things wherein they might edify one another '. There had been Societies of this kind formerly among the Puritans and Dissenters, but these new Religious Societies were within the Church of England. They engaged in social work, caring for the poor, and especially those who were in prison for debt, in addition to keeping up their own meetings for devotional fellowship. These, by the way, were often held in the vestries of the churches. The Societies raised funds to maintain clergy who read prayers at different churches at different hours, so that the devout could attend worship at any time of the day. Some of the Societies supported charity schools ; others devoted their efforts to the printing and distribution of religious books ; and others were active in reporting to the magistrates cases of drunkenness and profanity. Here, in fact, was the source of the various Societies for the Reformation of Manners, for the Propagation of Christian Knowledge, and so forth, which we encounter in the early years of the eighteenth century.

At the accession of James II the Religious Societies fell under suspicion, and to avert it some of them began to call themselves clubs, and hired a room in some quiet tavern where they could meet and maintain their religious fellowship. At the Revolution the Societies were once more free to carry on their work openly : this, and a new rule that was introduced about the same time binding every member to do his best to secure at least one new adherent, led to a very considerable increase in the numbers. The large growth of membership alarmed some people, who feared that the Societies would lead to a schism in the Church, and complaints were laid before the Bishop of London. The Societies formally vindicated themselves in a statement which declared that the only object in view was to quicken the religious life of the members, and to help them to live in all respects as worthy Christians. The bishop was satisfied, and said, ' God forbid that I should be against such excellent designs ! '

The elder Samuel Wesley had some knowledge of these Societies, and in 1699 he published *A Letter concerning the Religious Societies*, in which he warmly commends them, and wishes to see them established everywhere, since their sole design is ' to promote, in a regular manner, that which is the end of every

Christian, the glory of God, included in the welfare and salvation of themselves and their neighbours '. It is interesting to find John Wesley forming ' a little Society ' while he was in Georgia. He wrote in April, 1736 : ' Not finding, as yet, any door open for the pursuing our main design, we considered in what manner we might be most useful to the little flock at Savannah. And we agreed, (1) To advise the more serious among them to form themselves into a sort of little society, and to meet once or twice a week, in order to reprove, instruct, and exhort one another. (2) To select out of these a smaller number for a more intimate union with each other, which might be forwarded, partly by our conversing singly with each, and partly by inviting them all together to our house ; and this, accordingly, we determined to do every Sunday in the afternoon.'

Now, many of these Religious Societies in England existed in Wesley's early manhood, and there are numerous references in his *Journal* to occasions when he visited them. On Sunday, March 26, 1738, he tells us that he went to a Society in Oxford ' where (as my manner then was at all Societies) after using a collect or two and the Lord's Prayer, I expounded a chapter in the New Testament, and concluded with three or four more collects and a psalm '.

On the 23rd he spoke ' at Mr. Extell's Society'. On October 6 he ' began expounding at a little Society at Wapping '. On the 18th he ' met a Society (of soldiers chiefly) at Westminster '. It is immediately after this period of contact with the existing Religious Societies that Wesley formed the earliest Society of his own in England. It was on May 1, 1738, that Wesley inaugurated his first Society in London, acting on the advice of

Böhler.[1] It met first at James Hutton's house, and later moved to a room in Fetter Lane. This fellowship was clearly intended to be one of the Religious Societies on the usual model of those in London. It was not, at the time, expressly a Methodist Society, nor was it (as has been so often assumed) a Moravian Society. The Moravian congregation, which still possesses a chapel in Fetter Lane, was formally organized a little later. The chapel was leased by James Hutton from Lady Day in the year 1740. The United Societies of the People called Methodists date from ' the latter end of the year 1739 ', as Wesley expressly says. He states that at that time ' eight or ten persons came to me in London who appeared to be deeply convinced of sin, and earnestly groaning for redemption. They desired (as did two or three more the next day) that I would spend some time with them in prayer, and advise them how to flee from the wrath to come, which they saw continuously hanging over their heads. That we might have more time for this great work, I appointed a day when they might all come together, which from thenceforward they did every week, namely, on Thursday, in the evening. To these, and as many more as desired to join with them (for their number increased daily), I gave those advices, from time to time, which I judged most needful for them ; and we always concluded our meeting with prayer suited to their several necessities. This was the rise of the United Society, first in London, and then in other places '.[2] The fact is that there are three points which may

---

[1] The rules of this Society are given in Wesley's *Journal* under the date May 1, 1738. There is nothing in them about attendance at church or at the Communion, though probably these things were presupposed. There is a provision for Lovefeasts and Bands, which were both borrowed from the Moravians.

[2] Wesley's *Works*, VIII, p. 269.

Dᴍ

be regarded as the beginning of Methodism – the
first group of Methodists gathered around Charles
Wesley at Oxford in 1729 ; the Religious Society
formed in May 1738, which met in Fetter Lane ;
and the more formal organization of the United
Society in 1739.

Some of the usages of the earliest Methodist
Societies were borrowed from the Moravians, and
Wesley was in close association with Moravians for
some years. It was the contact with the Moravians
on board ship as he crossed the Atlantic, and in
Georgia, and the influence of Spangenberg, and
finally of Böhler, that led Wesley into the evangelical
experience of religion. Methodism owes more, in
fact, to Moravianism than to any other religious
movement. Now behind the Moravians, who
counted for so much in the experience of the
Wesleys, there was a long history, curious, and
rather obscure. The Apostle Paul says, in Romans
xv. 19, that he had fully preached the gospel of
Christ from Jerusalem, and round about even unto
Illyricum, and in 2 Timothy iv. 10 we read that
Titus had gone to Dalmatia. There is mention of
martyrs in these regions in the second and third
century. St. Jerome was a native of Stridon, on
the border of Dalmatia and Pannonia, and there is
a tradition that he translated the Bible into the
language of his countrymen. When the Slavs conquered these regions they found Christian churches
there, and it is recorded that some Slavonic bishops
refused to attend the sixth Ecumenical Council at
Constantinople in 680, because they disapproved
of the worship of images. It was in the ninth
century, however, that these Slavonic regions were
really evangelized by the apostolic labours of Cyril
and Methodius, who were Greek monks from
Thessalonica. Hence these lands were afterwards

in communion with the Eastern Church. A couple of generations later there was a pagan reaction. The Christians were persecuted and martyred, and King Wenceslaus of Bohemia was assassinated in the year 935 by his brother, who was still a heathen. Later, Christianity became the dominant religion, but the ecclesiastical affiliations were with the East rather than with the West. It is recorded that when a bishopric was established at Prague in 973 the Archbishop of Mainz would not install the first bishop until the Bohemians adopted the Latin rite. After this there was a protracted struggle, and apparently they were allowed for a time to revert to the Greek rite. There seem to have been vernacular services, too, and altogether Bohemia was never Romanized in the way that the rest of Western Europe was, until after the Reformation. The Emperor Charles IV in 1350 raised the see of Prague into an archbishopric, and established a university in the city. It seems to have been largely the influence of the university, with its German and Italian professors, which led to the more general acceptance of the Latin rite, along with clerical celibacy, the doctrine of transubstantiation, and the withdrawal of the chalice from the laity.

The great figure in the religious history of Bohemia is John Hus. He was prominent in the University of Prague, and in 1400 became the preacher at the Bethlehem Chapel, which had recently been built by a citizen of Prague, expressly for evangelical preaching in the vernacular. He became an advocate of Wyclif's doctrines, and by the irony of history it happens that Lollard teaching entered Bohemia partly as the result of a piece of Papal diplomacy. Charles V of France wanted to marry his son to Anne, the sister of Wenceslaus of Bohemia. But this was the period of the Papal

Schism, and France was in allegiance to Clement VII, the French Pope at Avignon, while England and Bohemia were in allegiance to Urban VI, the Pope at Rome. The Roman Pope, therefore, did his best to thwart the Bohemian alliance with France, and to promote the marriage between Anne of Bohemia and Richard II of England, which took place in 1382. In consequence, there was a good deal of intercourse between London and Prague, and some of the English visitors to Bohemia carried with them copies of Wyclif's writings. Presently these were translated into the vernacular and widely read in Bohemia. Another factor was the Hundred Years' War, in consequence of which many English students who could not go to the University at Paris went to that at Prague.

When Hus was burned at the Council of Constance in 1415 there was intense indignation in Bohemia, and for a time the country practically renounced allegiance to Rome. Later the Hussites developed differences among themselves ; there was a moderate party, the Calixtines, and a radical party, the Taborites. A religious war followed, in which Ziska defeated the crusading armies again and again. Then there were negotiations between the Council of Basle and the Bohemians, and a concordat between the Council and the Calixtines, known as the *Compactata*, which conceded the administration of the Eucharist in both species, and some other reforms, and which was in force for thirty years. The Taborites, however, were much more advanced than the Calixtines. When some of the citizens of Basle at the time of the Council went out of curiosity to witness a service conducted by Prokop, they were astonished to find that he used neither altar nor vestments, and that the whole service consisted of prayers, a sermon, and a simple Eucharist.

Rather later there came into existence, in a way that is obscure, but probably through developments among the Taborites, the community of the Bohemian Brethren, or *Unitas Fratrum*. There were sectaries called ' Brethren ' in many parts of Germany, toward the end of the thirteenth century, who passively resisted the priestly pretensions of the clergy, and professed a simple and evangelical creed. They held services in the vernacular, and also possessed versions of the Scriptures in their own language. On the express testimony of their persecutors they were distinguished for the purity of their lives. There was almost certainly a connexion between these groups of Brethren and the fellowships of prayer into which the followers of Eckhart, Tauler, Suso, and Ruysbroeck were gathered.

Now there was some relation between these Brethren and the Waldenses, and this, again, leads into some dim by-ways of ecclesiastical history. There appears to have survived into the Middle Ages, in some parts of Italy, especially Lombardy, an evangelical spirit which was opposed to the growing superstition in the Church. We know that Vigilantius, the opponent of Jerome, in his opposition to the cult of relics and images, the practice of pilgrimage, the celibacy of the clergy, and so forth, had the support of Lombard bishops. Claude, the Bishop of Turin in the early years of the ninth century, maintained a remarkable propaganda against the worship of images, the pretensions of the Roman see, and the growth of superstition generally. In the tenth century the letters of Hatto, the Bishop of Vercelli, indicate the existence of a considerable body of sectaries in the district who apparently maintained the evangelical protest.

It is difficult to resist the suspicion that there was

some connexion between anti-sacerdotal tendencies
such as these, and the existence of sects like the
Paterines of Milan, the Petrobusians and the
Henricians in the south of France, and the Waldenses, who were later found on both sides of the
Alps.   The Waldenses are supposed to derive their
name from Peter Waldo, a wealthy merchant of
Lyons, who (about the year 1170) became convinced that he ought to renounce the world, and
follow Christ and the apostles in a life of poverty.
He gave up his fortune to the poor, and speedily
gained disciples who did the same.   He sent them
forth two by two, preaching the gospel, with a
special emphasis on penitence and renunciation.
They were known as ' the Poor of Christ ', ' the
Poor Men of Lyons ', ' the Barefooted ' (*insabbati*),
and so forth.   Later on they were called Vaudois,
or Waldenses.   They were persecuted by the Archbishop of Lyons, and, upon his representations,
proscribed by the Council of Verona in 1184.   But
they went on with their evangelism, and within a
few years spread into Italy, Germany, and Spain.[1]

Many persecuted Waldenses found refuge in
Prague in 1418 and later.[2]   There were definite
negotiations between the Waldensians and the
Bohemian Brethren about 1467, and it is said that
Hardek, a Waldensian bishop, consecrated the first
bishop of the *Unitas Fratrum* about that time.   In
any case, there is no doubt that there was some considerable intercourse between the Waldenses and
the Bohemian Brethren.   One curious fact that
illustrates the close connexion between the Waldenses of Savoy and France, the Brethren of Germany,
and the *Unitas Fratrum* of Bohemia is that they all
used the same catechism for the instruction of their

---

[1] Lagarde, *The Latin Church in the Middle Ages*, pp. 109–10.
[2] Keller, *Die Reformation und die älteren Reformparteien*, p. 282.

children. This seems to have been printed first of all in 1498. It existed in French, Italian, German, and Bohemian.[1]

If any one man may be called the founder of the *Unitas Fratrum*, or Bohemian Brethren, it is Peter Chelčicky, a layman, who was born toward the end of the fourteenth century, and must have lived through the time of the Hussite wars. That may have influenced him in his thoroughgoing pacifism, in which he anticipated the Mennonites and the Quakers. He seems to have regarded himself as a disciple of Wyclif rather than of Hus, and was a strenuous enemy of Rome.

The Bohemian Brethren were very numerous in the fifteenth century. There was much persecution from time to time, and various attempts at reconciliation with the main body of the Utraquists. The Brethren made some approaches to Erasmus, who complimented them upon their knowledge of evangelical truth, but, characteristically, declined to commit himself further ; and also to Luther, who objected to some things in their beliefs and usages, especially their doctrine of the Eucharist, and their practice of rebaptism. The victory of Charles V over the forces of the Smalkaldic League at the battle of Mühlberg in 1547 led to renewed persecution, and many Brethren fled to Poland and Prussia. One of their bishops in the seventeenth century, John Amos Comenius, was an educational pioneer, and was consulted as to the reform of the English universities, which was under consideration in Parliament at the time. The scheme came to nothing, because of the outbreak of the war between the King and the Parliament, and Comenius returned to the Continent in 1642.

Then, in 1722, Johann Andreas Rothe, the pastor

[1] Lindsay, *History of the Reformation*, I, p. 155.

of Berthelsdorf, a village on the estate of Count Zinzendorf, in Upper Lusatia, brought to the notice of the Count a young Moravian, Christian David, who had been deputed by the persecuted Brethren to seek a place where they could settle in peace. The Brethren were being bitterly oppressed by the Catholic authorities in Moravia at the time, especially in the neighbourhood of Fullneck, which had formerly been the pastoral charge of Comenius. When David and his comrades came into Lusatia, Zinzendorf was away from home, and it was his grandmother, who was a Pietist, who assigned to the fugitives a place near the hill called the Hutberg, on the high road to Zittau, where they could settle. On June 17, 1722, Christian David, who was a carpenter, began to fell a tree to get timber for the dwelling, exclaiming as he struck the first blow with his axe, ' Here the sparrow hath found a house, and the swallow a nest for herself, where she may lay her young, even Thine altars, O Lord of Hosts ! ' Presently a village was founded, and named Herrnhut, ' the Watch of the Lord '.   The result was the development of a religious community distinguished by a warmth of evangelical feeling and a missionary zeal which made it extraordinarily influential in the days to come, in spite of the fact that it was never very large in numbers.   It was the example of the Moravians on board the ship that carried Wesley to America, and the influence of Spangenberg and Böhler, as we have seen, that counted for more than anything else in the decisive period of Wesley's religious experience.   It was in the Herrnhut *Gesangbuch* that Wesley found all the German hymns which he translated so magnificently into English. It was the Moravian system of groups for fellowship – ' Classes ' and ' Bands ' – that Wesley adopted, and that became characteristic of early

Methodism.[1] Two of the regular services that were held by the Methodists, the Lovefeast and the Watchnight, were also borrowed from the Moravians, and both were revivals of services held in the primitive Church, the *agapae* and the *vigiliae*.

Wesley was much influenced, in one way and another, by mysticism, and he owed this in part to the Moravians, but first of all to William Law. A great deal has been made (and a great deal too much, by some writers) of the influence of Law. Warburton was the author of the famous sneer that ' Law begat Methodism ', and this has been repeated by more responsible writers.[2] Charles Wesley was nearer the truth when he said, ' Mr. Law was our John the Baptist '.

The facts are quite simple. Law's *Christian Perfection* was published in 1726 and his *Serious Call to a Devout and Holy Life* in 1728, and Wesley studied these books constantly for the next few years, and

[1] Auch diese Unterabteilungen sind übernommen, übernommen von den Herrnhutern. Dort hatte man bekanntlich die ' Chöre ' der Verheirateten, der ledigen Schwestern, der ledigen Brüder, der Wittwen u.s.w., und innerhalb der einzelnen Chöre gab es auch dort sog. ' Banden ', d.h. Gesellschaften von 5-7 Personen eines Chores, die sich wöchentlich ein-oder zweimal in Gegenwart eines Helfers zusammenfanden, um sich über ihre religiösen Erfahrungen zu unterreden und so gegenseitig zu erbauen und zu fördern. – Loofs, ' Methodismus ', in Herzog-Hauck, *Realencyklopädie*, Heft 119, p. 769.

[2] Man hat William Law den Vater der englischen Erweckung des 18 Jahrhunderts und den Grossvater des Methodismus gennant. Mir scheint das weder geschmachtvoll, noch richtig. Aber das ist recht : wenn mann an die Verbreitung der ' Gesellschaften ' mit universaler ethisch-reformatorischer Tendenz und daran denkt, dass zugleich durch Law in den religiös suchenden Kreisen ein Ernst und ein Opfermut angeregt wurde, der mehr Kraft in sich hatte, als frommer Egoismus gebrauchte, so kann man verstehen, dass der Methodismus den Boden bereitet fand, als er in den religiösen Grundgedanken der Reformation ein Mittel der Selbsterbauung und universaler Einwirkung auf andere entdeckt hatte, das weder die *religious societies* Hornecks, noch die *societies for reformation of manners*, noch Law gekannt hatten. Loofs, ' Methodismus ', in Herzog-Hauck *Encyklopädie*, Heft 119, p. 752. It was Dr. G. A. Wauer, in *Die Anfänge der Brüderkirche in England*, who described William Law as ' the father of the English revival of the eighteenth century, and the grandfather of Methodism '. Wesley himself said of the earliest Methodists that there was ' some truth ' in Dr. Trapp's assertion that Mr. Law was their parent. Wesley's *Works*, VII, p. 203.

constantly recommended them and read them aloud to his friends. Thus we find him reading the *Christian Perfection* to the passengers on the *Simmonds* (as he records in his *Diary* on November 31, 1735), and to various people in Georgia later, Sophia Hopkey among the rest. He published an abridgement of the *Christian Perfection* in 1743, and of the *Serious Call* in 1744. He never lost his admiration for Law and these books of his, despite some sharp correspondence later on. ' It is true ', said Wesley, in a letter of September 17, 1760, ' that Mr. Law, whom I love and reverence now, was once a kind of oracle to me,' and as late as 1768 he published a volume of extracts from Law's later writings. He adopted some of Law's counsels as to methods of work and of devotion, and put them into practice in his own life, at least in his early days. He walked over from Oxford to Putney, first of all in 1732, and then on several later occasions, to consult Law. He asked Law's advice, too, when he was being urged to go to America, and did not receive much encouragement, for Law said that Wesley's plan in going to Georgia as a missionary to the Indians was the project of a ' crack-brained enthusiast '.

It was on Law's advice that Wesley began to study the mystics. The second time they met Law says that he put into Wesley's hands ' the little book of the *German Theology* ', and for the next few years Wesley diligently read the mystical writers. But after he had been brought face to face with the evangelical experience of religion by the challenge and counsel of men like Spangenberg and Böhler he came to feel that the mystics were deficient in their teaching as to the faith that saves, and he wrote to his brother Samuel from Georgia, ' I think the rock on which I had nearest made shipwreck of the faith was the writings of the Mystics '.

He felt the same defect in Law, and wrote a letter to him that we should feel to be arrogant, as from a young man to a much older one, if we did not remember that Wesley's love of plain dealing, and the extraordinary equanimity of his own temper, led him all his life long to deal with all sorts of people as frankly, not to say bluntly, as (to do him justice) he liked to be dealt with himself.

It has been the fate of John Wesley, again and again, to be misjudged on the ground of an uninformed interpretation of his own words. Undoubtedly this has been so in reference to mysticism. He said unkind things on many occasions about the ' mystic divines ', and this has led some writers to the conclusion that he had no sympathy whatever with mysticism. Leslie Stephen remarked that ' Mysticism seemed to John Wesley to be simply folly. His feet were on the solid earth, and he preferred the plain light of day to the glooms and glories loved by more imaginative natures'. A more inept judgement was never passed by a responsible writer.

The plain fact is that when Wesley condemned the mystics he had in mind some particular extravagances that were connected with the teaching of one or two men. He felt that Law, his old teacher, was deficient in his emphasis upon faith, and that this was due largely to the influence of the mystics, and he lamented the way that Law became an abject disciple of Boehme (or Behmen, as Wesley always calls him). He also strongly opposed the false quietism taught by Molther, which wrought so much havoc in the Society in London. One cannot wonder at these things.

Some of Boehme's writings are excellent specimens of mystical teaching, but some of them read like the ravings of a madman ; and Law had come

in his later years to regard almost every word that
Boehme had written as if it were inspired. Wesley
once commented sardonically on Boehme's exposition of the Lord's Prayer, in which some grotesque
significance is discovered, not only in every word,
but in every syllable, and that in the German !
' *Un* is God's eternal will to nature ; *ser* comprehends
in it the four forms of nature ; *va* is the matrix
upon the Cross ; *ter* is Mercury in the centre of
Nature.   And they are the two mothers in the
eternal will.   The one severs itself into fire, the
other into the light of meekness and into water.
For *va* is the mother of the light which affords
substantiality, and *ter* is the mother of the fire's
tincture.'   There are pages and pages of this stuff.
What is given here is merely the exposition of the
two words *Unser Vater*, ' Our Father '. Wesley was
surely excusable in saying that there must be ' a
very high degree of lunacy ' before any such drivel
could be written.

Then the perverse quietism which Molther taught
was enough to alarm and disgust anybody who was
really concerned about the souls of men.   ' Stillness ', with Molther and his followers, meant an
end of all effort and all discipline in the religious
life.   Those who were ' still ' called themselves ' poor
sinners ', or ' happy sinners ', and gave up prayer,
and the Sacraments, and the reading of the Bible,
because of the danger of trusting in these means of
grace.   Charles Wesley (who had himself been
almost carried away by ' stillness ' at one time)
wrote in his *Journal* in April 1740, ' The unjustified,
say they, are *to be still* ; that is, not to search the
Scriptures, not to pray, not to communicate, not to
do good, not to endeavour, not to desire ; for it is
impossible to use means without trusting in them.
Their practice is agreeable to their principles. Lazy

and proud themselves, bitter and censorious toward
others, they trample upon the ordinances and
despise the commands of Christ '.   These things
explain Wesley's unsympathetic utterances with
regard to mysticism.   It was what Wesley felt to be
the evangelical deficiency of many of the mystics,
and of William Law ; the demented theosophy
which so often spoils the writings of Boehme, and
which Law took so seriously ; and the dangerous
extravagances of Molther, with the dire results that
followed from them in practice, that led Wesley to
condemn ' the mystic scheme '.

But look at the other side of the question. Wesley
closely studied the *Theologia Germanica* on his voyage
to America in 1736, and read a *Life of Tauler* while
he was in Georgia.   There, too, he read the *Homilies*
of Macarius.   He quotes Macarius, by the way, in
the sermon on ' The Scripture Way of Salvation '.
He read Antoinette Bourignon's *Treatise of Solid
Virtue*, and her *Light of the World*, also while in
Georgia, and he published the former work in the
Christian Library in 1754.   He translated two of her
hymns, ' Venez, Jesus, mon salutaire ' (' Come,
Saviour Jesus, from above ') and ' Adieu, Monde,
vray pipeur ' (' World, adieu ! thou real cheat ! ').
He was acquainted with the writings of Pierre
Poiret, her biographer, and published extracts from
his *Instructions* in 1745.   In 1741 he published *An
Extract of the Life of Monsieur de Renty*, which he had
read in Georgia five years before.   In 1742 he read
Les Torrents Spirituels of Madame Guyon, and in
1756 he read her *Autobiography*.   In the Christian
Library he published at various dates the *Homilies*
of Macarius, the *Life of Gregory Lopez* (both of which
he had read in Georgia), the *Letters and Conversations
of Brother Lawrence*, the *Spiritual Letters* of Juan
d'Avila (the Spanish saint of whom St. Theresa

was a disciple), the *Pensées* of Pascal, some of the writings of John Smith and Henry More, the Cambridge Platonists, and *The Spiritual Guide* of Molinos, the Quietist (which A. H. Francke had translated into Latin in 1687). Consider the significance of these facts. It was rather unusual to find any sympathy with mystical teaching in the eighteenth century. There was no other edition of Molinos's book in England between 1699 and 1775, and I should not think that there was any other issue of the writings of Brother Lawrence in the eighteenth century. There had been considerable interest in the mystics during the Commonwealth, but (with the exception of William Law and Dr. Byrom and their devotion to Boehme) there was little knowledge of the mystical writers during Wesley's century. It might be seriously argued that Wesley stood almost alone in his age for his knowledge of some of the great mystics, and for his appreciation of what was best in them.

Wesley had read most of these mystical books while he was in Georgia, and it is true that the influence exerted upon him by the mystics dated generally from this early period of his life, but it must be remembered that he published some of these books in the Christian Library as late as 1756. Then the deeply mystical character of many of the hymns of Methodism should not be forgotten. Some of the very best of John Wesley's translations are from the hymns of Scheffler and Tersteegen, and it is plain that it was the mystical quality of these hymns that attracted him when he found them in the Herrnhut *Gesangbuch*, and led him to make his magnificent versions. Such are Scheffler's ' Du unvergleichlich Gut ' (' O God, of good the unfathom'd Sea ! ') and ' Ich will dich lieben, meine Stärke ' (' Thee will I love, my Strength, my

Tower ') and Tersteegen's ' Gott ist gegenwärtig '
(' Lo ! God is here : let us adore ') and ' Verborgne
Gottes Liebe du ' (' Thou hidden love of God,
whose height ').

It can hardly be denied, then, that Wesley and
early Methodism were considerably influenced,
directly and indirectly, by the mystics – at some
points by the study of great mystical books, and at
others by the strain of mystical teaching which
reached them through the Moravians and the
Pietists, and thus linked the religious revival in
England with an evangelical succession of doctrine
and experience reaching far back into the past.

CHAPTER III

WESLEY, METHODISM, AND THE CHURCH

THE whole question of the relation between Wesley, Methodism, and the historic Church is one of considerable interest. It is largely, of course, a matter of the connexion between Wesley and his followers on the one hand, and the Church of England on the other, but behind this there lies the whole question of Wesley's convictions as to the history, the authority, and the constitution of the universal Church.

Wesley described himself, on more than one occasion, as a High Churchman. It is true enough that many of his affinities were with the High Churchmen of that period, and it is also true that in his early clerical life there was a good deal that reminds one of the more extreme High Churchmen of to-day. When he was in Georgia, for example, he tried to carry out all the ritual regulations of the Church to the very letter, and brought some opposition upon himself as a result. He insisted on baptizing by immersion, even when the child was sickly, and he would accept none but communicants as sponsors. He refused to read the Burial Service over a Dissenter, and he would not admit Dissenters to the Holy Communion unless they were re-baptized. Years after all this, Wesley received a letter from John Martin Bolzius, one of the Moravians, which he inserted in his *Journal* under the

64

date September 29, 1749, with the comment, ' What a truly Christian piety and simplicity breathes in these lines ! And yet this very man, when I was at Savannah, did I refuse to admit to the Lord's Table, because he was not baptized – that is, not baptized by a minister who had been episcopally ordained. Can any one carry High Church zeal higher than this ? And how well have I since been beaten with mine own staff ! '

So far it is true, then, that Wesley was an eighteenth-century High Churchman in his early days. But when Anglican controversialists suggest that all his life he was a High Churchman, and in the modern sense, the term needs, to say the least, a good deal of very serious qualification. For one thing, Wesley (like most of the High Churchmen of the eighteenth century, indeed) was a thorough Protestant, and in this he was very unlike most of the High Anglicans of to-day. He did not deplore the Reformation and call it a disaster, as they often do. He wrote to Dr. Secker, the Bishop of Oxford, in 1748, ' It is the faith of our first Reformers which by the grace of God I preach '. He had no sort of sympathy with Roman usages. When he was at Mainz, in 1738, he copied out the notice of an indulgence which was posted on the door of the Cathedral, in the following terms : ' His Papal Holiness, Clement the XIIth, hath this year, 1738, on the 7th of August, most graciously privileged the Cathedral Church of St. Christopher, in Mentz ; so that every Priest, as well secular as regular, who will read mass at an altar for the soul of a Christian departed, on any holiday,[1] or on any day within the octave thereof, or on two extraordinary days, to be appointed by the Ordinary, of any week in the year, may each time deliver a soul out of the fire of

---

[1] So Wesley renders it : the German is *Seelentag*.

EM

Purgatory.' Wesley adds, ' Now I desire to know, whether any Romanist of common sense can either defend or approve of this ? ' He spoke again and again, in the strongest terms, about the idolatry and superstition of Romanists. In August 1739, when adverting to the charge that he himself was a Papist – a charge made, he says, generally either by ' bigoted Dissenters, or (I speak without fear or favour) ministers of our own Church ' – he takes occasion to quote a letter which he had written to a Catholic priest, giving his ' serious judgement concerning the Church of Rome '. In this he says that Romanists are guilty of ' adding to the things which are written in the Book of Life ', and specifies amongst these things the doctrines of the seven sacraments, of transubstantiation, and of purgatory ; and such practices as indulgences, prayer to the saints, the veneration of relics, and the worship of images, along with the claims made for the priority and universality of the Roman Church, and for the supremacy of the Pope.[1] On the Papal claims Wesley remarks, in the *Notes on the New Testament*, in his comment on 2 Thess. ii. 3, that while ' the man of sin, the son of perdition, eminently so called, is not come yet ', nevertheless ' in many respects the Pope has an indisputable claim to these titles ', since he ' increases all manner of sin above measure ', and ' has caused the death of innumerable multitudes ', and claims ' the prerogatives which belong to God alone '. In another place he says that the doctrines and practices which are peculiar to the Church of Rome ' were not instituted by Christ – they are unscriptural, novel corruptions '.[2] Elsewhere he speaks bitterly of the persecutions of which the Church of Rome has been guilty, and of ' that execrable slaughter-house, the Romish Inquisition ',

---

[1] Wesley's *Works*, I, pp. 219–21.   [2] Wesley's *Works*, III, p. 42.

and ' those holy butchers ' the inquisitors.[1]   In the
lines ' Written after Walking over Smithfield ',
Charles Wesley celebrates the ' glorious names ' of
the Protestant martyrs :

> Who nobly here for Jesus stood,
> Rejoiced, and clapp'd your hands in flames,
> And dared to seal the truth with blood !

In another hymn he describes the Church of Rome
as :

> that most straiten'd sect
> Who every other sect disown,
> Who all beside themselves reject,
> As heaven were bought for them alone.

Wesley and his brother were not, therefore, High
Churchmen in the modern sense, in so far as that
implies (as it so often does) the adoption of Roman
cults and usages, a wistful gaze directed toward
Rome with a hope of recognition and reunion, and
a general tendency to deprecate the Reformation.
Neither was Wesley, after his early days, a High
Churchman in any sacerdotal sense.   There is
ample proof of this in all his writings, but especially
in *The Sunday Service of the Methodists*, three editions
of which were issued – one, in 1784, for America,
and two others, in 1786 and 1788, for England.
This was Wesley's revision of the Book of Common
Prayer, and the very fact that he undertook such a
revision on his own responsibility is enough to give
pause to most High Anglicans.   The changes he
made are very significant indeed, though he himself
said in the Preface that he had made ' little alteration ' – which is also significant.   He goes on to
say that the principal changes he has made are
these – that ' most of the holy days (so-called) are

[1] Wesley's *Works*, VI, p. 480.

omitted as, at present, answering no valuable end ' ;
that the Sunday service is considerably shortened ;
that ' some sentences ' in the Offices of Baptism
and for the Burial of the Dead are omitted ; and
that many Psalms, and many parts of other Psalms,
are left out, ' as being highly improper for the
mouths of a Christian congregation '. But there are
many important changes besides these that are
specified in the Preface. The Absolution and the
Athanasian Creed disappear, and in every case
' minister ' or ' elder ' is substituted for ' priest '.
In the Order for Holy Communion, ' elder ' is used
instead of ' priest ', and in the Ordination Service,
instead of three forms for bishops, priests, and
deacons, there are three for ' superintendents ',
' elders ', and deacons. In Baptism the sign of the
cross is omitted, and also the sentence ' that it
hath pleased God to regenerate this infant with His
Holy Spirit '. The Order of Confirmation is left
out altogether, and so is the Order for the Visitation
of the Sick.

Then in 1784 Wesley abridged the Thirty-nine
Articles with the purpose of making a doctrinal
basis for the Methodist Societies in America. He
reduced the Articles to twenty-five in the process.
He took out of the article on baptism all reference
to any impartation of grace, and made it affirm that
baptism is a sign of the Christian profession, and
' also a sign of regeneration or the new birth '. Now
the significance of all this is plain.[1] The alterations
are exactly the kind of changes that would be made
by any evangelical Dissenter to-day if he had to

---

[1] Loofs remarks on Wesley's revision of the Thirty-nine Articles :
' Uebersieht man diese, so tritt zunächst ein Zweifaches hervor, das der
Methodismus nicht für sich allein hat, das aber doch von einzelnen Formen
des anglikanischen Christenthums ihn unterscheidet – der Gegensatz zu
allem Katholisieren und der Gegensatz zur Prädestinations-lehre und
dem, was mit ihr zusammenhängt.' – 'Methodismus ', in Herzog-Hauck
Encyklopädie, Heft 119, p. 799.

revise the Book of Common Prayer.   In fact, every single thing that has any trace of sacerdotalism or superstition is deleted.

It was at the same period in his life, in 1784, after the War of Independence, that Wesley wrote, ' As our American brethren are now totally disentangled, both from the State and from the English hierarchy, we dare not entangle them again, either with the one or the other.   They are now at full liberty simply to follow the Scriptures and the primitive Church.   And we judge it best that they should stand fast in that liberty wherewith God has so strangely made them free '.   Wesley would plainly have liked to see the Church of England, to which he was so sincerely attached, set free, not only from the remnants of sacerdotal doctrine in the Anglican formularies, but from the fetters of the Establishment and from the despotism of the bishops.   As early as 1739 he said in a letter to his brother Charles, referring to some of his critics who had quoted the passage of Scripture about submitting ourselves to every ordinance of man for the Lord's sake : ' True ; to every ordinance of man which is not contrary to the command of God.   But *if any man, bishop or other*, ordain that I shall not do what God commands me to do, to submit to that ordinance would be to obey man rather than God.'   When in 1758 a clergyman in the Isle of Man wished he could have offered Wesley his church, but explained that the bishop had forbidden him to do so, Wesley wrote : ' But is any clergyman obliged, either in law or conscience, to obey such a prohibition ?   By no means.   The will even of the King does not bind any English subject, unless it be seconded by an express law.   *How much less the will of a bishop ?*   " But did you not take an oath to obey him ? "   No, nor any clergyman in the three kingdoms. This is a mere vulgar error. Shame that it should prevail almost universally.'

We have seen that Wesley did not scruple to alter some of the services found in the Book of Common Prayer, and to omit others altogether. Neither did he scruple to introduce services not hitherto found in the worship of the Church of England, and some of these are specially interesting. Two were borrowed from the early Church, by way of the Moravians, and the other had its source in English Puritanism – I refer to the Lovefeast, the Watchnight, and the Covenant Service. In *A Plain Account of the People called Methodists*, Wesley gives the following statement as to the institution of the Lovefeast among the Societies : ' In order to increase in them a grateful sense of all God's mercies, I desired that one evening in a quarter all the men in Band, on a second, all the woman, would meet ; and on a third, both men and women together ; that we might together " eat bread ", as the ancient Christians did, " with gladness and singleness of heart ". At these Lovefeasts (so we termed them, retaining the name, as well as the thing, which was in use from the beginning) our food is only a little plain cake and water. But we seldom return from them without being fed, not only with " the meat which perisheth ", but with " that which endureth to everlasting life ".'[1]

Wesley records that a remarkable Lovefeast was held at Fetter Lane on January 1, 1739, when ' about three in the morning, as we were continuing instant in prayer, the power of God came mightily upon us, insomuch that many cried out for exceeding joy, and many fell to the ground. As soon as we were recovered a little from that awe and amazement at the presence of the Divine Majesty,

[1] Wesley's *Works*, VIII, pp. 258–9.

we broke out with one voice, *We praise Thee, O God ;
we acknowledge Thee to be the Lord !* ' (A few lines
before this Wesley records that ' we had the blessed
Sacrament every day this week, and were comforted
on every side ' – a passage that is constantly
quoted by Anglo-Catholic writers as a proof of
Wesley's devotion to the Eucharist. Why do they
not quote the other passage in proof of his devotion
to the Lovefeast ?)

Wesley gives an account of the origin of the
Watchnight in *A Plain Account of the People called
Methodists*. He writes : ' About this time I was
informed that several persons in Kingswood frequently met together at the school ; and, when
they could spare the time, spent the greater part of
the night in prayer, and praise, and thanksgiving.
Some advised me to put an end to this ; but, upon
weighing the thing thoroughly, and comparing it
with the practice of the ancient Christians, I could
see no cause to forbid it. Rather, I believed it
might be made of more general use. So I sent
them word, I designed to watch with them on the
Friday nearest the full moon, that we might have
light thither and back again. I gave public notice
of this the Sunday before, and, withal, that I
intended to preach ; desiring they, and they only,
would meet me there, who could do it without prejudice to their business or families. On Friday
abundance of people came. I began preaching
between eight and nine ; and we continued until a
little beyond the noon of night, singing, praying,
and praising God.

' This we have continued to do once a month
ever since, in Bristol, London, and Newcastle, as
well as Kingswood ; and exceeding great are the
blessings we have found therein. It has generally
been an extremely solemn season ; when the Word of

God sunk deep into the heart, even of those who till then knew Him not. If it be said, " This was only owing to the novelty of the thing (the circumstance which still draws such multitudes together at those seasons), or perhaps to the awful silence of the night " : I am not careful to answer this matter. Be it so : however, the impression then made on many souls has never since been effaced. Now allowing that God did make use either of the novelty or any other indifferent circumstance, in order to bring sinners to repentance, yet they are brought. And herein let us rejoice together.

' Nay, may I not put the case farther yet ? If I can probably conjecture, that, either by the novelty of this ancient custom, or by any other indifferent circumstance, it is in my power to " save a soul from death, and hide a multitude of sins ", am I clear before God if I do it not, if I do not snatch that brand out of the burning ? '[1]

Wesley records in his *Journal* that the first Watch-night was held in London on April 9, 1742. He adds : ' We commonly chose for this solemn service the Friday night nearest the full moon,[2] either before or after, that those of the congregation who live at a distance may have light to their several homes. The service begins at half-an-hour past eight, and continues till a little after midnight. We have often found a peculiar blessing at these seasons.'

In *A Letter to the Reverend Mr. Baily of Cork*[3] – a reply to an attack that this clergyman had made on his activities – Wesley writes : ' You charge me, fourthly, with holding " midnight assemblies ". Sir, did you never see the word Vigil in your

[1] Wesley's *Works*, VIII, pp. 255–6.
[2] In these days the Watchnight Service is only held on the last night of the year, and many other Churches have copied the usage from the Methodists.
[3] Wesley's *Works*, IX, p. 81.

Common Prayer Book? Do you know what it means? If not, permit me to tell you, that it was customary with the ancient Christians to spend whole nights in prayer ; and that these nights were termed *Vigiliae*, or Vigils. Therefore for spending a part of some nights in this manner, in public and solemn prayer, we have not only the authority of our own national Church, but of the universal Church, in the earliest ages.'

Wesley has left an account in his *Journal*, under the dates August 6 and 11, 1755, of what is apparently the first institution of the Covenant Service. On Wednesday, the 6th, he writes : ' I mentioned to the congregation [i.e. in London] another means of increasing serious religion, which had been frequently practised by our forefathers, and attended with eminent blessing ; namely, the joining in a covenant to serve God with all our heart and with all our soul. I explained this for several mornings following, and on Friday many of us kept a fast unto the Lord, beseeching Him to give us wisdom and strength to promise unto the Lord our God and keep it.' Then on the 11th he writes : ' I explained once more the nature of such an engagement, and the manner of doing it acceptably to God. At six in the evening we met for the purpose in the French Church in Spitalfields. After I had recited the tenor of the covenant proposed, in the words of that blessed man, Richard Alleine,[1] all the people

---

[1] Richard Alleine (1611–1681) was the son of a clergyman of the same name who was Rector of Ditcheat, in Somerset. He was educated at Oxford, first at St. Alban's Hall, and then at New Inn. He became Rector of Batcombe, and was ejected in 1662. He died at Frome Selwood. He wrote *Vindiciae Pietatis*, which was published in 1663. Joseph Alleine (1634–1668) was also educated at Oxford, first at Lincoln College, where John Wesley later held his Fellowship, and then at Corpus Christi. He became assistant pastor at Taunton, a great centre of Puritanism. (John Wesley evidently remembered this association with Taunton, for on September 2, 1789, he wrote in his *Journal* : ' When we set out one of my horses was quite lame, so that it was with great difficulty I could get to

stood up, in testimony of assent, to the number of about eighteen hundred persons. Such a night I scarce ever saw before. Surely the fruit of it shall remain for ever.' In April 1757 he writes in the *Journal*, ' On Good Friday, in the evening, at the meeting of the Society, God was eminently present with us. I read over and enlarged upon Joseph Alleine's *Directions for a Thorough Conversion to God* '. The service for the Renewal of the Covenant was held on the following Monday at Spitalfields, with about twelve hundred people present. ' At half-hour after nine, God broke in mightily upon the congregation.'

There are many references in the *Journal* to the remarkable blessing which attended this particular service whenever it was held. Thus Wesley writes on July 12, 1778, during the meeting of the Conference, ' We solemnly renewed our covenant with God. It was a time never to be forgotten. God poured down upon the assembly the spirit of grace and supplication, especially in singing that verse of the concluding hymn :

> To each the covenant blood apply,
> 　Which takes our sins away ;
> And register our names on high,
> 　And keep us to that day ! '

Taunton. In the evening we had such a congregation as, I suppose, was never in that house before. Surely the ancient work will some time revive, and the prayers of that blessed man Joseph Alleine, be answered.' Joseph Alleine married a daughter of Richard Alleine, who appears to have been a relative. He was ejected in 1662. After this he exercised a wandering ministry as an evangelist (in which he was associated with Wesley's grandfather, who was also, of course, an ejected minister). Alleine was much persecuted, and spent several terms in prison. *The Alarm to the Unconverted* appeared in 1672, and it is stated that more than seventy thousand copies of it were sold within the next three or four years. Wesley published an extract from it in the *Christian Library*, and he also issued three editions of Alleine's *Christian Letters*. It appears to be a mistake to attribute the source of the Covenant Service to Richard Alleine. It derives from *Joseph* Alleine and the error arose through the *Vindiciae Pietatis* being bound up with some writings of Joseph Alleine.

And he records, again and again, on these occasions,
' a great blessing ', ' a peculiar blessing ', ' an un-
common blessing ', ' God was with us, of a truth ',
' the Spirit of glory and of God rested upon us ',
' many received the pardoning love of God, or
power to love Him with all their heart '.

Now, as Wesley himself pointed out, the Lovefeasts were a renewal of the *agapae* and the Watch-
nights a renewal of the *vigiliae* of the primitive
Church. He found authority in the Scriptures for
the Covenant Service, in passages like Deuteronomy
xxvi. 17–18, Jeremiah xxxi. 31–4, and Ezekiel xvi.
60, and he called it ' a Scriptural means of grace which
is now almost everywhere forgotten, except among
the Methodists '. But none of these services was a
revival with any antiquarian or ritualistic motive
behind it. These rites were found useful and effective in bringing sinners to God and in confirming
the devotion of believers, and that was justification
enough in the eyes of Wesley. Was this a revival of
a usage in the early Church, and that the invention
of Puritans a century before ? It did not matter
either way, as long as both were used and blessed
of God.

In short, Wesley could find Scriptural and traditional authority for other usages besides the two
Sacraments, but he never based any rites whatever
upon such authority alone ; the last reason why
he urged all these things upon his people was that
there was spiritual good to be found in them. As
a matter of fact, God had continually blessed all
these ordinances to believers, and so they were
warranted by the witness of His Spirit in the experience of His people.

We have seen that Wesley showed a good deal
of independence and of initiative with regard to the
rites and regulations that were traditional in the

Church of England. It is also to be noted that he did not accept any general doctrine of the Church that would satisfy a High Anglican of to-day, or, indeed, any one but a convinced Evangelical. He held that the Church of Christ is the whole body of real believers in the world, apart from any particular organization, or any historical succession except, of course, the succession of an experience of redemption, continually renewed within the fellowship of believers by the grace of God. The Church consists of all those who have a living faith in Christ, whatever they are called by themselves or by others. In the words of Charles Wesley, it is ' the Church of pardoned sinners, Exulting in their Saviour '.

Thus, when discussing the relation of the Methodists to the Church of England, John Wesley writes : ' What, then, do they mean who say, " You separate from the Church " ? We cannot certainly tell. Perhaps they have no determinate meaning ; unless by the Church they mean themselves, i.e. that part of the clergy who accuse us of preaching false doctrine. And it is sure we do herein separate from them, by maintaining the doctrine which they deny. " But do you not weaken the Church ? " Do not they who ask this, by the Church mean themselves ? We do not purposely weaken any man's hands, but accidentally we may thus far – they who come to know the truth by us, will esteem such as deny it less than they did before. But *the Church, in the proper sense, the congregation of English believers*, we do not weaken at all.' So Wesley writes again, in one of his sermons : ' The catholic or universal Church is, all the persons in the universe whom God hath so called out of the world as to entitle them to the preceding character ; as to be one body, united by the one Spirit ; having one faith, one hope, one baptism, one God and Father of all, Who is above all, and through all, and in them all. . . . *Two or three Christian believers united together are a Church in the narrowest sense of the word.*[1]

In 1761 Wesley wrote, and published in the *London Chronicle*, an answer to a pamphlet entitled *A Caveat against the Methodists*. In this he defines the conception of the Church thus : ' I answer, It is true, " all these promises, prophecies, and characters, point out a society founded by Christ Himself, and by His commission propagated throughout the world, which should flourish till time should end " : And such is the Catholic church, that is, *the whole body of men, endued with faith working by love, dispersed over the whole earth*, in Europe, Asia, Africa, and America. And this church is " ever one " : In all ages and nations it is the one body of Christ. It is " ever holy " ; for no unholy man can possibly be a member of it. It is " ever orthodox ", so is every holy man, in all things necessary to salvation : " Secured against error ", in things essential, " by the perpetual presence of Christ ; and ever directed by the Spirit of truth ", in the truth that is after godliness. This church has a " perpetual succession of Pastors and Teachers, divinely appointed, and divinely assisted ". And there has never been wanting in the Reformed Churches, such a succession of Pastors and Teachers ; *men both divinely appointed, and divinely assisted ; for they convert sinners to God* : A work none can do unless God Himself doth appoint them thereto ; and assist them therein ; therefore every part of this character is applicable to them. Their Teachers are the proper successors of those who have delivered down, through all generations, the faith once delivered to the saints ; and their members have true spiritual communion with the " one holy " society of true believers ;

1 Wesley's *Works*, VI, pp. 395–6.

consequently, although they are not the whole " people of God ", yet they are an undeniable part of His people.'

In 1746 Wesley read *An Inquiry into the Constitution, Discipline, Unity, and Worship of the Primitive Church*, by Peter King, who eventually became Lord Chancellor, and died in 1734. Wesley wrote : ' In spite of the vehement prejudice of my education, I was ready to believe that this was a fair and impartial draught, but if so, it would follow that bishops and presbyters are essentially of one order, and that, originally, every Christian congregation was a church independent of all others.' The influence of King's book appears very plainly at the next Conference, for the *Minutes* of 1747, in discussing the constitution of the Church, conclude that there must be, in the nature of things, numberless accidental varieties in the government of the various Churches ; that it was because the wisdom of God had regard to this necessary variety that there is no determinate plan of Church government appointed in Scripture ; and that there was no thought of uniformity in the government of the Church until the time of Constantine, ' and would not have been then, had men consulted the word of God only '. This is an unquestionable fact of history : it was only political pressure and ecclesiastical ambition, directed from Constantinople and Rome, that first attempted to create a single, uniform, and exclusive organization in the Church.

Wesley had no exaggerated respect (to say the least) for the Church of the Fathers. He wrote in his *Journal* on August 5, 1754 : ' I set out for Canterbury. On the way I read Mr. Baxter's *History of the Councils*. It is utterly astonishing, and would be wholly incredible, but that his vouchers are beyond all exception. What a company of execrable wretches they have been (one cannot justly give them a milder title), who have almost in every age, since St. Cyprian, taken upon them to govern the Church ! How has one Council been perpetually cursing another ; and delivering all over to Satan, whether predecessors or contemporaries, who did not implicitly receive their determinations, though generally trifling, sometimes false, and frequently unintelligible, or self-contradictory ! Surely Mahometanism was let loose to reform the Christians ! I know not but Constantinople has gained by the change.'

Wesley had no doctrinaire beliefs with regard to the Church and its authority and its ordinances, in fact. His whole attitude was pragmatic. If anything that was traditional in the Church worked effectively, and made for the salvation of souls, well and good ; if it did not, he was prepared to let it go. He said so, in so many words, in a letter to Dr. Secker, the Bishop of Oxford, dated June 25, 1746 : ' Methinks I would go deeper. I would inquire what is the end of all ecclesiastical order ? Is it not to bring souls from the power of Satan to God and to build them up in fear and love ? Order, then, is so far valuable as it answers these ends ; and if it answers them not, it is nothing worth.'

In exactly the same strain Wesley once said to the Bishop of London, ' Church or no Church, we must attend to the work of saving souls ' ; and at another time he remarked summarily, ' If we must either dissent or be silent, *actum est* '. He had, in fact, apart from the Calvinistic doctrine of the Dissenters generally (and in some cases their Antinomian doctrine), no such blind horror of Dissent as most eighteenth-century Churchmen had. He chanced to preach for the last time before the University of Oxford on St. Bartholomew's Day, August 24, 1744.

When he was writing *A Short History of the People called Methodists* in 1781, thirty-seven years later, he recalled the significance of the date, and said, ' I am well pleased that it should be the very day on which, in the last century, near two thousand burning and shining lights were put out at one stroke '. Both of Wesley's grandfathers were of the number ejected in 1662.

In a purely technical and legal sense the Methodists *were* Dissenters. Charles Wesley lamented to William Grimshaw in a letter dated March 27, 1760 : ' Our preaching-houses are mostly licensed, and so are proper meeting-houses. Our preachers are mostly licensed, and so are Dissenting Ministers. They took out their licences as Protestant Dissenters.' But this was done, of course, to escape the fines which might be levied under the Conventicle Act, and also to protect the meeting-houses from the violence of mobs. The Riot Act of 1715 contained a clause making it felony to demolish, or attempt to demolish, any building erected for the purposes of religious worship which was certified and registered under the Toleration Act of 1689, and the Act declares that compensation may be recovered from the hundred in which the building is situate, if the building is destroyed, or damaged.[1]

The protection given by such registration of preachers and chapels was not always effective, because it was often held by justices that as Methodists attended the parish churches, they were not Dissenters, and therefore could not avail themselves as Dissenters of the relief given by the Toleration Act. In a letter addressed by Wesley to ' A Member of Parliament ' (who was probably Wilberforce) in July 1790, he quotes two recent instances

[1] J. S. Simon, *John Wesley the Master Builder*, p. 77.

of this kind of injustice.   A man in whose house a Methodist service had been conducted was arraigned and fined £20, and a preacher was arrested and fined £20.   The registration of the building and the licence of the preacher were held to be void, on the ground that the Methodists could have no relief under the Act of Toleration, because they went to church.   Wesley says in the letter, ' Now, sir, what can the Methodists do ?   They are liable to be ruined by the Conventicle Act, and they have no relief from the Act of Toleration ! '

With regard to the Sacraments of the Church, Wesley's attitude was mainly pragmatic.   He found that, as a matter of fact, these hallowed rites brought blessing to the believing soul, and therefore he urged them upon his people.   That is the truth, and practically the whole truth, of the matter.   It is, of course, easy enough to make out that Wesley was a sacramentarian if you go through his writings and select and stress every reference to the duty of receiving the Holy Communion, and the blessing which attends it.   But it creates an entirely false impression if you isolate those references, and give them a unique emphasis.   He accepted the two Sacraments on the authority of the Scriptures as of our Lord's institution, of course, but he certainly did not attribute to them any magical efficacy. A great deal that has been written on Wesley's supposed sacramentarianism is entirely beside the mark, and a good deal of it is rather disingenuous. It is easy to quote a multitude of references as to the duty and privilege of attendance at the Lord's Supper.   It would be equally easy to quote as many allusions (or, indeed, more) to the duty and privilege of attending meetings for preaching and prayer and fellowship, and the good that such attendance brought with it.   Wesley often tells the

FM

Methodists in general, and some of his corre-
spondents in particular, that if they neglect to attend
their Classes and Bands it will be at the peril of
their souls' salvation. Wesley regarded the cultiva-
tion of spiritual fellowship in these groups as a vital
thing – as vital as any other ordinance of the
Church. No one goes through Wesley's *Journal*
with a magnifying-glass to discover and enumerate
and emphasize all the references he made to the
solemn duty of attending the preaching service at
five o'clock in the morning, and the blessing which
attended that ordinance – he said more than once
that Methodism would perish if the five o'clock
preaching were neglected or given up.[1] But every
such reference to the Holy Communion is dwelt
upon in the effort to show that John Wesley was a
sort of Anglo-Catholic. He was nothing of the sort,
as all his life and all his writings show. There are
innumerable passages in which Wesley stresses the
uselessness, and even the danger, of every form and
every rite apart from the spiritual conditions, the
penitence and faith and devotion in the heart,
which alone can make it into a means of grace.

As early as 1726, when Wesley had been preaching at Stanton, he made reference in his *Diary* to a
subsequent conversation with Mrs. Pendarves:
' Talked of the nature of a Sacrament. *Much harm is
done by exaggerating the venerableness of it.* Proposing
it as an object of fear rather than love deters multitudes from receiving it.' Again and again in later
life he guards against any *ex opere operato* doctrine.
In the sermon on ' The Means of Grace ' he writes :
' Whosoever imagines there is any intrinsic power in
any means whatsoever, does greatly err, not knowing the Scriptures, neither the power of God. We
know that there is no inherent power in the words

---

[1] Wesley's *Works*, IV, pp. 267, 269.

that are spoken in prayer, in the letter of Scripture read, the sound thereof heard, or the bread and wine received in the Lord's Supper ; but that it is God alone Who is the Giver of every good gift, the Author of all grace ; that the whole power is of Him, whereby, through any of these, there is any blessing conveyed to our souls. *We know, likewise, that He is able to give the same grace, though there were no means on the face of the earth.* In this sense, we may affirm, that, with regard to God, there is no such thing as means ; seeing He is equally able to work whatsoever pleaseth Him, by any, or none at all.'[1] Later on, at the end of the same sermon, he writes : ' Remember also, to use all means, *as means ; as ordained, not for their own sake, but in order to the renewal of your soul in righteousness and true holiness. If, there-fore, they actually tend to this, well ; but if not, they are dung and dross.'*

In his sermon on ' The Way to the Kingdom ' Wesley writes : ' True religion does not consist in any . . . ritual observances ; *nor indeed on any outward thing whatever ; in anything exterior to the heart ;* the whole substance thereof lying in righteousness, peace, and joy in the Holy Ghost. *Not in any outward thing, such as forms, or ceremonies, even of the most excellent kind.* Supposing these to be ever so decent and significant, ever so expressive of inward things, supposing them ever so helpful, not only to the vulgar, whose thought reaches little farther than their sight, but even to men of understanding, men of stronger capacities, as doubtless they may some-times be ; yea, supposing them, as in the case of the Jews, appointed by God Himself ; yet even during the period of time wherein that appointment remains in force, true religion does not principally consist therein ; *nay, strictly speaking, not at all. . . .*

[1] Wesley's *Works*, V, pp. 188–9.

The religion of Christ rises infinitely higher, and lies immensely deeper, than all these. These are good in their place ; just so far as they are in fact subservient to true religion. And it were superstition to object against them, when they are applied only as occasional helps to human weakness. *But let no man carry them farther. Let no man dream that they have any intrinsic worth, or that religion cannot subsist without them.* This were to make them an abomination to the Lord.'[1]

In his specific references to the Sacraments of Baptism and the Lord's Supper, Wesley's teaching is quite as definite as in his wider allusions to rites and ordinances in general. We have seen that he took out of the Book of Common Prayer all reference to baptismal regeneration. In the *Notes on the New Testament*, commenting on Romans ii. 25, *If thou art a transgressor of the law, thy circumcision is become uncircumcision*, Wesley remarks : ' Is so already, in effect. Thou wilt have no more benefit by it, than if thou hadst never received it. The very same observation holds with regard to baptism.' In his sermon on ' The Marks of the New Birth ' he writes : ' Say not then in your heart, " I was once baptized ; therefore I am now a child of God ". Alas, that consequence will by no means hold. How many are the baptized gluttons and drunkards, the baptized liars and common swearers, the baptized railers and evil-speakers, the baptized whoremongers, thieves, extortioners ? What think you ? Are these now children of God ? '[2]

Wesley's teaching as to the nature of the Lord's Supper is equally unmistakable : the bread and the wine are a sign, a seal, a figure, a memorial. In the *Notes on the New Testament* he comments on Luke xii. 19, 20, *This is My body* – ' As He had just now

[1] Wesley's *Works*, V, pp. 77–8.   [2] Wesley's *Works*, V, p. 221.

celebrated the Paschal supper, which was called the
Passover, so in the like figurative language, He calls
this bread His body. And this circumstance of itself
was sufficient to prevent any mistake, as if this bread
was his real body, any more than the Paschal lamb
was really the Passover. *This cup is the New Testament* – Here is an undeniable figure, whereby the
cup is put for the wine in the cup. And this is called
The New Testament in Christ's blood, which could not
possibly mean that it was the New Testament itself
but only the seal of it, and the sign of that blood
which was shed to confirm it'. So also on Matthew
xxvi. 26–8, *Take, eat; this is My body . . . This is My
blood . . .* Wesley's comment is, ' *This* bread *is,* that is,
signifies or represents *My body . . . This is* the sign of
My blood '. And on Mark xiv. 24, *This is My blood
of the New Testament,* ' That is, this I appoint to be a
perpetual sign and memorial of My blood, as shed
for establishing the New Covenant '.

We have seen that Wesley held a thoroughly
evangelical view of the whole doctrine of the Church
and of the Sacraments. That view conditioned his
entire attitude toward a separation between the
Methodists and the Church of England. The whole
question looks at first sight a good deal more entangled than it really is. There appears to be an
inevitable inconsistency in the words and acts of a
man who is steadily being forced into a position he
does not want and does not like. Wesley did not
wish the Methodists to leave the Church of England,
and said so again and again, in the strongest terms.
Yet for fifty years he was steadily preparing for the
separation which he often deprecated, and yet
sometimes admitted to be almost inevitable.
Charles Wesley was ' a more stationary man ', as Dr.
Johnson said, than his brother. He was much more
of a Churchman ; much more jealous of the

Methodist preachers developing into a regular
ministry ; and he was much more nervous at the
prospect of a separation. As he said himself, with
perfect truth, ' All the difference between my
brother and me was that my brother's first object
was the Methodists and then the Church : mine
was first the Church and then the Methodists'.[1] In
fact, John Wesley's whole position in the matter is as
well illustrated by his brother's marked reluctance
and repeated remonstrances as by anything that
happened in the whole history of the question.

The issue came into prominence in very early
days. In the *Minutes* of 1744 the following statement occurs : ' Q. Do you not entail a schism
on the Church ? that is, Is it not probable that
your hearers, after your death, will be scattered into
all sects and parties ? or that they will form themselves into a distinct sect ? A. (1) We are persuaded the body of our hearers will, even after our
death, remain in the Church, unless they be thrust
out. (2) We believe, notwithstanding, either that
they will be thrust out, or that they will leaven the
whole Church. (3) We do, and will do, all we can,
to prevent those consequences, which are supposed
likely to happen after our death. (4) But we
cannot, with a good conscience, neglect the present
opportunity of saving souls while we live, for fear
of consequences which may possibly or probably
happen after we are dead.'

In the *Minutes* of 1747 there is the following :
' Q. Are not the Methodists guilty of making a
schism on the Church ? A. No more than rebellion or murder. They do not divide themselves at
all from the living body of Christ. Let any prove it,
if they can.'

On the nature of schism Wesley expressed himself

---

[1] Quoted in *The Letters of John Wesley*, VIII, p. 267.

more than once, in the plainest terms, and as a matter of interpretation he was unquestionably right. He points out in the sermon ' On Schism ' that ' heresy ' and ' schism ' in the New Testament mean the same thing – ' divisions, or parties, *in* a religious community ', and not ' a separation *from* any Church or body of Christians, with or without cause '.[1] In the *Notes on the New Testament,* in his comment on I Corinthians xi. 13 – *I hear there are schisms among you* – Wesley remarks : ' It is plain that by *schisms* is not meant any *separation* from the Church, but uncharitable *divisions* in it. For the Corinthians continued to be one Church, and notwithstanding all their strife and contention, there was no separation of any one party from the rest, with regard to external communion. And it is in the same sense that the word is used in i. 10 and xii. 25, which are the only places in the New Testament beside this, where *church-schisms* are mentioned. Therefore, the indulging any temper contrary to this tender care of each other, is the true scriptural *schism*. This is therefore quite a different thing from that orderly separation from corrupt churches, which later ages have stigmatized as *schism*, and have made a pretence for the vilest cruelties, oppressions and murders, that have troubled the Christian world. . . . Both *heresy* and *schism*, in the modern sense of the words, are sins that the Scripture knows nothing of ; but were invented merely to deprive mankind of the benefit of private judgement, and liberty of conscience.' Wesley, therefore, would not have admitted that a separation from the Church of England entailed the sin of schism. The strongest thing he ever said about separation – a dictum which Anglo-Catholic controversialists delight to quote – occurs in a letter to Samuel Bradburn, dated

[1] Wesley's *Works*, VI, pp. 404–5.

March 25, 1783 : ' I still think when the Methodists leave the Church of England, God will leave them.' But Anglo-Catholics do not often quote the sentences that immediately follow. ' Every year more and more of the clergy are convinced of the truth, and grow well affected toward us. It would be contrary to all common sense, as well as to a good conscience, to make a separation *now*.' Wesley's whole point is that evangelical religion was gaining ground in the Church of England, that more clergymen were in sympathy with the Methodists, and that therefore any formal separation was unwise and uncharitable at such a juncture, whatever it might have been, or might yet be, under other conditions.

All Wesley's utterances on this issue may be well enough understood, contradictory as they often seem, if we remember his own paradoxical position – that he was a clergyman, called of God to be the leader of a great religious revival which was welcomed by a few, disliked by most, and brutally opposed by many, of the clergy of his own Church. He kept on all his life hoping to see an evangelical revival within the Church of England that should transform it. When he thought he discerned signs of such a change of heart, he rejoiced, and was more than ever reluctant to see a separation ; when he was brought up against shameful opposition to the Methodists on the part of the clergy, and mere formalism and utter irreligion in the Church, he despaired, and thought that the separation would come, and must come, in spite of all that he could do.

All this may be amply illustrated from Wesley's own utterances on the subject. Thus in 1786 he wrote to Thomas Taylor regarding the possibility of a separation from the Church of England, and stating his belief that if the Methodists had left the

Church years before they would not have done a
tenth of the good that had been done. 'But I do not
insist upon this head. I go calmly and quietly on
my way, doing what I conceive to be the will of
God. I do not, will not, concern myself with what
will be done when I am dead. I take no thought
about that.' In his pamphlet on *Thoughts on Separation from the Church*, which was written in 1778,
Wesley says that ' the question properly refers to *a
total and immediate separation. . . . Such* a separation I
have always declared against ; and certainly it will
not take place (if ever it does) while I live. But *a
kind of separation has already taken place, and will
inevitably spread, though by slow degrees.*'[1] At the
Conference of 1788 Dr. Coke proposed that the
Methodists should formally separate from the
Church of England. Dr. Adam Clarke relates that
when Coke had ended his argument, Wesley rose
and said calmly, ' Dr. Coke would *tear* all from top
to bottom ; I will not tear, but *unstitch* ! ' Samuel
Bradburn, one of Wesley's preachers, reports that
Wesley once remarked : ' As soon as I am dead the
Methodists will be a regular Presbyterian Church.'[2]

The whole position cannot be summed up better
than in the words of Dr. Rigg : ' Looking at the
whole evidence, it appears to be undeniable that, so
far as respects the separate development of Methodism, Wesley not only pointed but paved the way to
all that has since been done, and that the utmost
divergence of Methodism from the Church of
England at this day is but the prolongation of a line
the beginning of which was traced by Wesley's own
hand. It is idle to attempt to purge Wesley of the
sin of schism in order to cast the guilt upon his

[1] Wesley's *Works*, XIII, p. 230.
[2] In his pamphlet, *The Question, Are the Methodists Dissenters ? Fairly
Examined*, p. 15.

followers. There is, indeed, neither sin, nor, properly understood, schism in the case, unless it be that the sin of persecution and proscription may be chargeable on some of the ministers and people of the Church of England. But at any rate Wesley himself led his people into the course which they have since consistently pursued. It is, at the same time, no less undeniable that separation was the necessary result of Wesley's work, because the Church of England failed to make any provision – in fact it made no effort toward providing – for the incorporation of Methodism within its own system.'[1]

It must be remembered that for fifty years Wesley was trying to hold his followers to the Church, and that all that time there were numberless things in the Church, and numberless acts by the clergy of the Church, that were repelling them from it. 'I am a Church of England man,' said Wesley in his old age, 'and, as I said fifty years ago, so I say still, in the Church I will live and die, unless I am thrust out.' He was not thrust out, but his people were. Many of them had no inherited loyalty to the Church such as he had. Multitudes of them had been reclaimed from a life of utter ungodliness by the preaching of the Methodists ; they owed all that they had to Methodism, and they gave all their loyalty to it. They could not be expected to tolerate the formalism and irreligion of the Church, and the active persecution they suffered from it, with the patience and loyalty and equanimity that Wesley generally showed. It is a wonder that he bore it as he did. It would be impossible to quote the hundreds of examples which are found in the *Journal* of the sort of thing meant. Here are a few. In the early days of the movement – it was in 1740 – Charles Caspar Graves, one of

---

[1] *The Churchmanship of John Wesley*, p. 109.

the Oxford Methodists, had to sign a letter at the behest of the Fellows of Magdalen, in which he solemnly renounced ' the practice of the Methodists ', which was defined as ' preaching in fields, assembling together and expounding the Holy Scriptures in private houses, and elsewhere than in churches . . . and their pretensions to an extraordinary inspiration and inward feeling of the Holy Spirit '. Two years later he recanted this with shame and contrition. When Wesley had his famous interview with Butler, who was Bishop of Bristol, that prelate – far and away the ablest man, and also one of the best and most devout on the bench of bishops – said to him, ' You have no business here, you are not commissioned to preach in this diocese. Therefore I advise you to go hence '. Wesley answered, ' My lord, my business on earth is to do what good I can. Wherever, therefore, I think I can do most good, there must I stay, as long as I think so. At present I think I can do most good here ; therefore, here I stay '.

This was the kind of treatment which the early Methodists received from the Universities and the bishops. It was followed by long years in which the churches were closed against them, and the foulest slanders circulated about them, by the parish clergy, and in which there were numberless examples of mob violence, where the rioters were led by the local clergyman, often ' warm from the alehouse '. When Wesley is describing the wonderful results of the preaching of the Methodists, in *A Farther Appeal to Men of Reason and Religion*, he urges that the clergy ought to have received the Methodist preachers ' with open arms ; and to have taken them who had just begun to serve God into their peculiar care ; watching over them in tender love, lest they should fall back into the snare of the devil.   Instead of this, the greater part spoke of those ministers as if the devil, not God, had sent them.   Some repelled them from the Lord's Table ; others stirred up the people against them, representing them, even in their public discourses, as fellows not fit to live ; Papists, heretics, traitors ; conspirators against their King and country.   And how did they watch over the sinners lately reformed ? Even as a leopard watcheth over his prey.   They drove some of them also from the Lord's table ; to which till now they had no desire to approach. They preached all manner of evil concerning them, openly cursing them in the name of the Lord.   They turned many out of their work ; persuaded others to do so too, and harassed them all manner of ways '. In the later years of Wesley's life there was less of physical violence, but there was still a great deal of clerical rancour.   Thus he records that he went to the parish church at Scarborough on June 20, 1784, and heard the vicar make a bitter attack on Methodism.   He remarks in his *Journal* : ' So all I have done to persuade the people to attend the church is overturned at once !   And all who preach thus, *will drive the Methodists from the church, in spite of all that I can do.*'   Four years later he visited the home of his childhood once more, and he records in his *Journal*, on July 6, 1788 : ' I came to Epworth, but was sorry to see scarce twenty communicants, half of whom came on my account.   I was informed, likewise, that scarce fifty persons used to attend the Sunday service.   What can be done to remedy this sore evil ?   I would fain prevent the members here from leaving the Church ; but I cannot do it.   As Mr. G. is not a pious man, but rather an enemy to piety, who frequently preaches against the truth, and those that hold and love it, I cannot, with all my influence, persuade them either to hear him or to attend the Sacrament administered by him. *If I cannot carry this point while I live, who then can do it when I die ?* And the case of Epworth is the case of every church where the minister neither loves nor preaches the Gospel. The Methodists will not attend his ministrations. What, then, is to be done?'

One of the points mentioned in this last passage is a most important factor in the matter of separation from the Church of England, and in Wesley's ordination of some of his preachers, which technically made the separation an accomplished fact. Wesley could not persuade the Methodists of Epworth to attend the Holy Communion administered by an ungodly clergyman. This particular issue occurred in a great many places. Is it to be wondered at that the Methodists did not care to take the Communion from the hands of a cleric who was a worldling, a drunkard, a man of notoriously unclean life ? Is it to be wondered at that they wished to receive it from the hands of their own preachers, to whom they owed their very souls – men who had given up their lives to the preaching of the gospel and the pastorate of souls, and who were, in all but a purely technical sense, separated and appointed to the work of the ministry ? In a letter to his brother Charles, dated June 20, 1755, Wesley refers to the question of administration by the preachers – the issue had arisen in Ireland – and says : ' Do you not understand that they all promised by Thomas Walsh not to administer, even among themselves ? I think that a huge point given up ; *perhaps more than they could give up with a clear conscience.*' The whole question was being discussed throughout the country at this time, and the feeling in favour of administration by the preachers was especially strong in the North of England. A few of the preachers, without waiting for the decision of the Conference, began to administer the Sacrament of the Lord's Supper in some of the Societies. There is a passage in Charles Wesley's shorthand diary which throws light on the situation. He says, in October 1754, that he had heard of Charles Perronet giving the Communion in the Minories and of Walsh giving it at Reading. Then the diary proceeds : ' *October 19.* – I was with my brother, who said nothing of Perronet except " We have in effect ordained already ". He urged me to sign the preachers' certificates ; was inclined to lay on hands; and to let the preachers administer. *October 24.* – Was with my brother. He is wavering ; but willing to wait before he ordains or separate.'

A few years later Charles Wesley writes to William Grimshaw, on March 27, 1760 : ' Three of our steadiest preachers give the Sacrament at Norwich, with no other ordination or authority than a sixpenny license. *My brother approves of it. All the rest will most probably follow their example.*'[1]

It was the active persecution of Wesley's followers by the clergy for long years, but still more the unworthiness of the lives of many clerics, which was an offence to godly Methodists at all times, but which became peculiarly distressing when they were expected to receive the Holy Communion at the hands of such men – it was this sort of thing, multiplied by the score all over England, by which the Methodists were (in Wesley's phrase) ' thrust out ' of the Church. He saw the approaching result, deplored it, resisted it, and finally accepted it, as his words and actions prove. The last act in his reluctant acceptance of the position was his ordination of some of his preachers. Wesley tells us that he had read Lord Chancellor King's book on *The Primitive Church* in 1746, and it convinced him that

[1] Jackson, *Life of Charles Wesley,* II, p. 187.

' the uninterrupted succession ' was ' a fable which no man ever did or can prove ', and that ' bishops and presbyters are of the same order, and consequently have the same right to ordain '. He tells us, again, that he believed episcopacy to be ' scriptural and apostolical – I mean, well agreeing with the practice and writings of the Apostles. But that it is prescribed in Scripture I do not believe. This opinion, which I once zealously espoused, I have been heartily ashamed of ever since I read Bishop Stillingfleet's *Irenicon*'. This book convinced him that ' neither Christ nor His Apostles prescribe any particular form of Church government'. As every one knows, modern scholarship has absolutely endorsed the convictions at which Wesley thus arrived. We know quite definitely that ἐπίσκοπος and πρεσβύτερος were used indifferently for the same person and the same office in the New Testament and in the earliest days of the Church, and we can trace both the gradual development of the episcopate into a separate order, and the melancholy growth of sacerdotal notions, in the few centuries that followed. Now, a man who said that apostolical succession was a fable, who held that bishops and presbyters are of the same order, and who ' firmly believed ' that he himself was ' a Scriptural ἐπίσκοπος as much as any man in England or in Europe ',[1] surely cannot be called a High Churchman in any sense in which the phrase is generally employed to-day.

The famous sermon on ' The Ministerial Office ', published in 1789 in the *Arminian Magazine*, is made much of by High Anglican controversialists. They forget both the occasion of the sermon and much of the language in it. Some of the preachers in Ireland had begun to give the Holy Communion,

[1] Wesley's *Works*, XIII, p. 220.

entirely on their own authority, and Wesley asks,
' Did *we ever appoint you* to administer Sacraments ?
. . . where did *I appoint you* to do this ?   Nowhere at
all ! '   The charge is not that they were not episcopally ordained, or that they were not ordained (in
the usual sense of the word) at all, but that they had
not been ordained or commissioned by Wesley himself to administer the Sacrament.   At this very
period he was ordaining or commissioning others of
his preachers to do this very thing.

Wesley once remarked that soul-damning clergymen laid him under more difficulties than soul-
saving laymen.[1]   He said in a letter to Alexander
Mather, ' Give me one hundred preachers who fear
nothing but sin, and desire nothing but God, and
I care not a straw whether they be clergymen or laymen,
such alone will shake the gates of Hell and set up
the kingdom of heaven upon earth '.   It is notice-
able, therefore, that Wesley would not have held
the distinction between the cleric and the layman
to be nearly as vital or important as most Anglicans
would, either then or now.   As early as 1745 he
wrote to ' a serious Clergyman ', ' I think he is a
true evangelical minister, διάκονος, " servant " of
Christ and His Church, who οὕτως διακονεῖ, " so
ministers " as to save souls from death, to reclaim
sinners from their sins ; and that every Christian,
if he is able to do it, has authority to save a dying
soul '.[2]   Here, as always with Wesley, the final test
is a practical one.   He wrote in the sermon on ' A
Caution against Bigotry ', ' But what if a man has
these (i.e. a holy life, and the necessary gifts for the
ministry) and has brought sinners to repentance,
and yet the Bishop will not ordain him ?   Then the
Bishop does forbid him to cast out devils.   But *I*

[1] *Arminian Magazine* (1779), p. 375.
[2] *The Letters of John Wesley* (edited by Dr. Eayrs), p. 111.

dare not forbid him . . . lest I be found even to fight against God '.[1]

The question of ordination became urgent after the American War. The Methodists in America had for years past demanded that their preachers should administer the Sacraments, and they had been held back by Asbury, in deference to Wesley's known reluctance. But now the Church of England had practically ceased to exist in America. Wesley entreated the Bishop of London, on at least two occasions, to ordain some of the Methodist preachers for America, but the request was refused. Finally, on September 20, 1780, Wesley ordained Richard Whatcoat and Thomas Vasey as presbyters, and Dr. Coke as superintendent, for the American Societies. Charles Wesley was horrified. He said that it was an action that would lead to ' a schism as causeless and unprovoked as the American rebellion ' – surely an unfortunate parallel in the light of history ! He also wrote the celebrated squib :

> How easily are bishops made
> By man or woman's whim !
> Wesley his hands on Coke hath laid,
> But who laid hands on him ?

In 1785 Wesley ordained three of his preachers for Scotland. These preachers were not allowed to administer the Holy Communion when they crossed the border and came into England. Odd as this seems, there were parallels in the early Church, which may perhaps comfort, or else perturb, the souls of the ecclesiastically minded. In the Canons of the Council of Chalcedon (VI) it is provided that ordination became invalid if the person ordained were not designated for service in some particular church.[2]

[1] Wesley's *Works*, V, p. 489.
[2] Hatch, *The Organization of the Early Christian Churches*, p. 138.

GM

When Wesley was referring to his ordination of three preachers for Scotland he said that this had nothing to do, naturally, with a separation from the Church of England. ' I have no thought of this ; I have many objections against it. . . . " But for all this, *is it not possible there may be such a separation after you are dead ? "* *Undoubtedly it is.* But what I said at our first Conference above forty years ago, I say still : " I dare not omit doing what good I can while I live, for fear of evils that may follow when I am dead ".'[1]

Then in 1789 Wesley ordained three of the preachers for England. He did not use the word ' ordain ' or the word ' bishop ' on any of these occasions, but these eight men were appointed ' presbyters ', and Dr. Coke (who was already a presbyter of the Church of England) ' Superintendent ', which, in view of the facts, can only mean *episcopus.*

I do not suppose that any Methodist to-day is much concerned about any criticism or any defence of Wesley's action in these ordinations, as regards any respect of ' validity '. Wesley's own position in the matter evidently amounted to this. He believed that his own preachers, since they were called of God and used of God in the actual work of the ministry, as preachers and pastors, were really ministers of the Church in all but a formal appointment, or ordination. He preferred episcopal ordination, as he said himself, ' when it could be had ', but he frankly recognized, on many occasions, the orders of Lutheran and Presbyterian ministers. Since the bishops would not ordain his preachers, and since he regarded himself as a scriptural ἐπίσκοπος, he himself ordained them. It was logical enough from his own point of view, for he evidently

[1] Tyerman, *Life of Wesley*, II, p. 442.

believed that all his preachers lacked of the clerical character was some regular appointment as ministers by some responsible authority. He gave them that formal appointment himself, and if John Wesley had not enough spiritual authority to do it, I can only say, for my own part, that I cannot imagine that any man in England at that time, or at any other time, had more, or, indeed, anything like as much.

CHAPTER IV

THE RELIGIOUS CONTRIBUTION

On the occasion of the centenary of Wesley's death, in 1891, *The Times* had a leading article which remarked, with real discernment, that the commemoration was ' even more significant for the gradual absorption which the last one hundred years have witnessed of the essential spirit of Wesley's teaching into the common religious life and social effort of the community than for the remarkable expansion of Methodism proper throughout the religious world '. It is this fact that makes the difficulty in any attempt to assess the contribution of Methodism to the religious life of the English-speaking peoples. A great deal that might be claimed, and properly claimed, as part of that contribution would readily pass to-day, with those who do not know the eighteenth century well, as merely the commonplaces of religion, and especially of evangelical religion. But all this was not commonplace in 1738. Much of the very essence of Christianity, as at least all evangelical Christians conceive it, had passed out of the religious life ; what all the Reformers, and most earnest souls from the Reformation down to the time of the Commonwealth, understood and experienced, had apparently become unintelligible to the people in England who supposed themselves religious in the first half of the eighteenth century.

There are some reasons for this which may be

readily seen. The rigidity of Puritanism had provoked a reaction, all the more violent because
Puritanism had been politically dominant. At the
Restoration the revulsion against Cromwell and the
Commonwealth, though first of all a political
episode, had also expressed itself in part as a scornful
repudiation of Puritan religion. The welter of
queer sects and the element of religious extravaganza during the Commonwealth, made possible
by Cromwell's policy of toleration, had also provided matter for ridicule in the hands of satirists
like Butler, and so the Puritan type of religion was
further discredited. Then, somewhat later, Arian
and Socinian doctrine had emasculated much of the
older Nonconformity : an illustration of which
process is to be found in the fact that all the churches
that survive to-day from the dominant Presby-
terianism of the Commonwealth are Unitarian.
Then, again, Deism was the ruling type of thought
in the region of religious philosophy during the first
years of the eighteenth century. Christianity was
regarded, both by friends and foes, as little more
than natural religion – either natural religion en-
cumbered with miracles and superstition, of which
the more radical thinkers wished to rid it, or natural
religion reinforced by miracles and revelation, as the
apologists of the time sought to argue, but in either
case little more than a system of morality, with or
without some tincture of the supernatural. All the
wonder and mystery and paradox of religion were
utterly discounted, in any case.

The result of all this was that there was less vitality
and less reality in English religion, in the early years
of the eighteenth century, than at any period, perhaps, in English history. Many acute observers, both
native and foreign, remarked upon the fact that religion was almost entirely discredited in England in

that generation. Hume said that the English people had ' settled into the most cool indifference with regard to religious matters that is to be found in any nation in the world '. Bishop Butler remarked, in a well-known passage, ' It has come, I know not how, to be taken for granted, by many persons, that Christianity is not so much as a subject of inquiry, but that it is now at length discovered to be fictitious. And accordingly they treat it as if, in the present age, this were an agreed point among all people of discernment, and nothing remained but to set it up as a principal subject of mirth and ridicule, as it were by way of reprisals, for its having so long interrupted the pleasures of the world '. Both Montesquieu and Voltaire, as observers of English life from a foreigner's point of view, remarked on the way that religion had become merely a matter of ridicule in England, especially among the upper classes.

The state of the Church was lamentable, as the religious temper of the time would lead us to expect. Bishop Butler refused the Primacy in 1747 on the ground that ' it was too late for him to try to support a falling Church ', and the best men in the Church were almost in despair as to its condition, as they well might be. Bishop Burnet wrote in 1713 : ' Our ember weeks are the burden and grief of my life. The much greater part of those who come to be ordained are ignorant to a degree not to be apprehended by those who are not obliged to know it. The easiest part of knowledge is that to which they are the greatest strangers : I mean the plainest parts of the Scriptures. They can give no account, or at least a very imperfect one, of the contents of the Gospels, or of the Catechism itself.' There is ample evidence in Wesley's own writings, as well as everywhere else in eighteenth-century literature, as to the utter debasement of many of the clergy.

The state of religion, then, was deplorable in every sense. Many of the standard facts of Christian life and Christian experience were distrusted, or ignored, or explained away, in a fashion that it is difficult for us to realize, unless we know a good deal about the temper of eighteenth-century religion. Take the fact of conversion as an example. Probably no one on the bench of bishops to-day would be really shocked or scandalized at the story of some sudden and remarkable conversion, but an eighteenth-century prelate would most certainly have been deeply disgusted. He would have regarded such a narrative as the delusion of a wild enthusiast, and a horrid pretension to the extraordinary gifts of the Holy Ghost, and so on. To-day religious people of every community recognize that the phenomena of conversion really happen, and eminent psychologists make elaborate studies of such experiences. Even the man in the street would hardly deny that there are such religious facts, whatever may be the explanation of them. But the typical Churchman of the middle of the eighteenth century did not believe that things of this kind happened at all, or that they ought to happen. He had a horror of fanaticism, and anything beyond going to Church, taking the Holy Communion, and living a moral life, savoured of ' enthusiasm '. The change in the meaning of that word is alone enough to illustrate the change of temper. To-day it means eagerness and energy of spirit ; in Wesley's time it meant wild delusions and religious frenzy.[1]

[1] In *A Farther Appeal to Men of Reason and Religion* (*Works*, VIII, p. 105) Wesley wrote : ' I could not well understand for many years how it was that on the mentioning of any of these great truths, even among men of

It is true that in some few cases in the early days of Methodism there were strange phenomena, on the border of the physical and the psychical, which accompanied instances of sudden conversions, and attracted adverse comment. Such things, again, do happen ; I have seen them happen occasionally myself. When the next great revival of religion comes, they will probably happen again, as they have always done in the past. There are records of such strange facts by scores in the lives of the saints in every age, and in the history of every period of religious revival, from early Christianity to the first days of the Franciscan movement, and from then to the Welsh Revival of 1905. It is easy to make far too much of such things. They are mere epiphenomena.

It was not accompaniments of this kind that counted for very much in the dislike of eighteenth-century churchmen for Methodism. It was much more the fact that real experiences of conversion happened, and that they happened suddenly. In our own days Dr. Inge has put it on record that ' he had never met with a case even remotely resembling the sudden conversions that the Methodists are led to expect '. But some of us have seen many instances of sudden conversion, where no one in his own senses could possibly doubt that a spiritual change of an amazing kind had really taken place in a moment, and where the reality of it has

education, the cry immediately arose, " An enthusiast ! An enthusiast ! " But I now plainly perceive this is only an old fallacy in a new shape. To object *enthusiasm* to any person or doctrine is but a decent method of begging the question. It generally spares the objector the trouble of reasoning, and is a shorter and easier way of carrying his cause. . . . I believe thinking men mean by *enthusiasm* a sort of religious madness ; a false imagination of being inspired by God ; and by an *enthusiast* one that *fancies* himself under the influence of the Holy Ghost, when, in fact, he is not. Let him prove me guilty of this who can. I will tell you once more the whole of my belief on these heads ; and if any man will show me (by arguments, not hard names) what is wrong, I will thank God and him.'

been witnessed by a changed life for many years afterward, as long as the man lived. When a man who has been a drunkard, a gambler, a cruel husband, and a brutal father, immoral and profligate in all the relationships of life, repents, believes, casts himself upon the mercy of God in Christ, and finds an assurance of pardon and peace, all in an hour, as it seems (though the Spirit of God has doubtless been at work in the man's heart long before), and when that man for the next thirty or forty years lives the life of a real Christian, pure, humble, devout, and kind – there can surely be no doubt as to what has happened. That happens still, though not so often as it ought to do, and it happened to thousands of men in the early days of Methodism.

Not that the experience is always sudden, nor that the early Methodists expected it to be. This is a point of some importance. It has been constantly assumed by some critics of Methodism that Wesley and his followers expected every one who really became a Christian to pass through a sort of standardized type of sudden conversion. That was not so. In Wesley's own experience there was a moment when he received a new assurance of the mercy of God, but there was no drastic change in his moral attitude or his moral behaviour. He had been a real Christian before, but without the sense of pardon and peace that is a Christian's privilege. In the lives of many other men who had been profligates there was a sudden moral change as well, and that seems to be inevitable, for if a man who has been living a life of sheer immorality becomes a disciple of Christ, there must be a moment when he breaks with his past. In most instances, even where the life has been externally blameless, there is probably some high instant of decision and surrender, and in many (as in Wesley's case) some memorable moment when the pardoning love of God is realized as it was never realized before.

But Wesley did not insist upon the suddenness of any religious experience as the vital thing. He wrote to Lady Maxwell in July 1765 : ' It may please God to give you the consciousness of His favour, the conviction that you are accepted through the Beloved, by almost insensible degrees like the dawning of the day ! And it is all one how it began, so you do but walk in the light. Be this given in an instant, or by degrees, hold it fast. Christ is yours ! He hath loved you, and hath given Himself for you.' To another correspondent he wrote, ' Permit me likewise to add one thing more : be the change instantaneous or gradual, see that you never rest till it is wrought in your own soul, if you desire to dwell with God in glory '. As a matter of fact, the emphasis with Wesley was, as it has been with his followers since, much more upon the definiteness than upon the suddenness of the experience.

But it was not only the fact of conversion, sudden or otherwise, that was strange to the religious thought of the early eighteenth century. The whole conception of religion had lost all its high lights, and had been reduced to a matter of moral behaviour and a decent observance of the external rites of religion. A multitude of references in Wesley's writings show the type of so-called religion against which he had to witness. What is holiness ? he asks. ' Not a bare external religion, a round of outward duties, how many soever they be, and how exactly soever performed.' What is faith ? he asks. ' Not a barely speculative, rational thing, a cold, lifeless assent, a train of ideas in the head ; but also a disposition of the heart.' What, he asks, is generally accounted religion ? and he answers : ' (1) The doing no harm, the abstaining from outward sin ; at least from such as is scandalous, as robbery, theft, swearing, drunkenness. (2) The doing good, the relieving the poor ; the being charitable, as it is called. (3) The using the means of grace ; at least the going to church and to the Lord's Supper. He in whom these three marks are found is termed by the world a religious man.'[1] In another sermon Wesley says : ' Very many write and preach as if Christian holiness, or religion, were a purely negative thing ; as if not to curse and swear, not to lie or slander, not to be a drunkard, a thief, or a whore-monger, not to speak or to do evil, was religion enough to entitle a man to heaven ! How many, if they go something further than this, describe it only as an outward thing ! as if it consisted chiefly, if not wholly, in doing good (as it is called) and using the means of grace ! Or, should they go a little further still, yet what do they add to this poor account of religion ? Why, perhaps, that a man should be orthodox in his opinions, and have a zeal for the constitution in Church and State. And this is all. This is all the religion they can allow, without degenerating into enthusiasm ! '[2]

That was the popular view of what was meant by religion. But even the few who took the religious life with the utmost seriousness and sincerity had a conception of it that was extremely unevangelical. It became a life of prolonged penance, in fact ; by penitence and prayer and self-discipline and self-denial, maintained to the end, a man might hope to deserve pardon at the last day, though he could never be sure of it until then. There was thus no

[1] Wesley's *Works*, V, p. 9, p. 268.
[2] Wesley's *Works*, VII, p. 456.

deep confidence in the soul, for there was no present sense of forgiveness bestowed by a pardoning God in His boundless grace upon the sinner who has cast himself upon the everlasting mercy in Christ. Therefore there was little sense either of peace or of joy in the life of the soul.

This might be endlessly illustrated. Think, for example, of the devotional manuals that were in vogue. There were no devotional books which exercised a wider influence in the eighteenth century than Jeremy Taylor's *Holy Living* and *Holy Dying*, and the volumes represent the best type of Anglican piety in that age. Though Taylor died some thirty years before Wesley was born, his influence as a devotional writer was certainly greater in the period of Wesley's earlier life than it had ever been before, or perhaps has ever been since. Here is a very characteristic passage from the *Holy Living* (IX. viii. 9) : ' No man is to reckon his pardon immediately upon his returns from sin to the beginnings of a good life, but is to begin his hopes and degrees of confidence according as sin dies in him, and grace lives, as the habits of sin lessen, and righteousness grows. . . . For we must know that God pardons our sins by parts ; as our duty increases, and our care is more prudent and active, so God's anger decreases. . . . *And whether God hath forgiven us or no, we know not, and how far we know not,* and all that we have done is not of sufficient worth to obtain pardon ; therefore still pray, and still be sorrowful for having done it, and for ever watch against it ; and then those beginnings of pardon which are working all the way, will at last be perfected in the day of the Lord.' That is to say, no man has a right to claim the forgiveness of his sins by simply casting himself on the mercy of God in Christ, but if he repents and prays and lives a righteous life he may *hope* for pardon, and, indeed, may have an increasing hope as the righteousness of his life increases, but he can never be sure that his penitence and his righteousness are sufficient, and so he can never be sure of pardon.

How far this is from the spirit of the New Testament ! The central message of the Gospel is that God in Christ forgives the penitent sinner who does not deserve forgiveness, and cannot deserve forgiveness. The pardoning mercy of God has no relation whatever to a man's righteousness, at that point. ' Christ Jesus came into the world to save *sinners*.' The sinner is saved by grace ; his pardon and his righteousness are alike effected by the grace of God. Whatever goodness there may subsequently be in his life is as much the gift of God as the fact of his pardon, and his righteous deeds are not presented to God to merit His forgiveness for the past, but are the fruit of the experience of renewal which always accompanies the experience of pardon. The forgiven sinner rejoices to make his life a living sacrifice in the service of God, with no thought whatever of winning pardon by it, but in thankfulness for the pardon God has already given, and freely given, in Christ. The good deeds of a believer's life are done utterly without any thought of deserving anything. Indeed, it is of the essence of the Gospel that man cannot deserve anything of God. ' For merit lives from man to man, But not from man, O God, to Thee ! '

There is a striking letter written by John Gambold, and addressed to Charles Wesley, on January 23, 1738, which vividly illustrates the religious temper of the time. He says that he has lately come to see, more than ever he could have imagined, ' how intolerable the doctrine of faith is to the mind of man, and how peculiarly intolerable to religious

men. One may say the most unchristian things,
even down to Deism ; the most enthusiastic things,
so they proceed but upon mental raptures ; the
most severe things, even the whole rigour of ascetic
mortification, and all this will be forgiven. But if
you speak of faith in such a manner as makes Christ
a Saviour to the uttermost ; as discovers a greater
pollution in the best of us than we could before
acknowledge, but brings a greater deliverance from
it than we could before expect – if any one offers to
talk at this rate, he shall be heard with the same
abhorrence as if he was going to rob mankind of
their salvation '.[1] This is the offence of the gospel
in every age, but it seems to have been peculiarly
repellent to the people of that particular period.
The natural man, in St. Paul's sense of the word,
does not like to be told that he is a sinner ; that,
however moral his life may have been outwardly,
he needs to be saved from the sinfulness and
selfishness that is within his heart ; and that he can
only be saved from it by a humble acceptance of the
redeeming grace of God in Christ, on exactly the
same terms as the vilest among men, if they also
repent and believe. That was what was new and
strange and unwelcome to the nominally religious
man when Methodism began its course. What !
said he, am I, who have always lived a moral life,
and gone regularly to church every Sunday, and
taken the Communion once a month, and read the
Bible and believed the Creed – am I to be told that
I must be saved exactly on the same terms as a
penitent felon in Newgate ? He did not see that his
was really an attitude of self-satisfaction and self-
righteousness, which bars the way into the Kingdom
of God as effectually as any act of sin. The early
Methodists were near the heart of the gospel when

[1] Tyerman, *The Oxford Methodists*, p. 169.

they sang, ' Whate'er obstructs Thy pardoning love, Or sin, *or righteousness*, remove, And take it all away ! '

It may be noted here that the very passage from Taylor's *Holy Living* that has been quoted above attracted Wesley's attention while he was at Oxford, and even then he felt that it was evangelically deficient. He referred to it in a letter to his mother dated June 18, 1725. ' In treating of repentance he says, " Whether God has forgiven us or no, we know not ; therefore be sorrowful for ever having sinned ". I take the more notice of this last sentence because it seems to contradict his own words in the next section, where he says that by the Lord's Supper all the members are united to one another, and to Christ the Head. The Holy Ghost confers on us the graces necessary for, and our souls receive the seeds of, an immortal nature. Now surely these graces are not of so little force as that we cannot perceive whether we have them or no ; if we dwell in Christ, and Christ in us, which He will not do unless we are regenerate, *certainly we must be sensible of it*. . . . If we can never have any certainty of our being in a state of salvation, good reason it is that every moment should be spent, not in joy, but in fear and trembling ; and then, undoubtedly in this life, we are of all men most miserable ! God deliver us from such a fearful expectation as this ! Humility is undoubtedly necessary to salvation ; and if all these things are essential to humility, who can be humble, who can be saved ? '

What Wesley already felt, even in the early period of his life, to be the evangelical defect in Jeremy Taylor, who was so representative of the age as a devotional writer, might be illustrated again and again from the religious life of Wesley's own contemporaries. Dr. Johnson is as good an example as

any. John Wesley and Samuel Johnson were unquestionably the most interesting personalities of
the period. They were close contemporaries, for
Johnson was only six years Wesley's junior, and
he died only seven years before Wesley.   On
December 18, 1783, Wesley visited Johnson for the
last time, and wrote in his *Journal* : ' I spent two
hours with that great man, Dr. Johnson, who is
sinking into the grave by a gentle decay.'   This
must have been the last of many visits, though,
strangely enough, it is the only one that Wesley
records. But the way in which Johnson refers to
Wesley's conversational gifts clearly implies that
they had met frequently. ' John Wesley's conversation is good,' said Johnson on one occasion, ' but
he is never at leisure. He is always obliged to go
at a certain hour. This is very disagreeable to a
man who loves to fold his legs and have out his talk,
as I do.'   At another time Johnson said of Wesley,
' He can talk well on any subject ', and then,
through a remark of Boswell's, the conversation
diverged on to the subject of ghosts, by way of a
reference to the story which Wesley inserted in his
Journal under the date of May 25, 1768. Boswell
was interested in this story, in addition to being
eager at all times to make the acquaintance of a
great man. So he asked Johnson to give him a
letter of introduction to Wesley. Boswell presented
this when Wesley was at Edinburgh, and says that
he was very politely received, but adds that he was
not satisfied with the evidence about the ghost.   It
is very characteristic that Boswell asked for the
letter of introduction to be given back to him, and
got it ! One of Johnson's references to Wesley, by
the way, though unmistakable enough, has not
been identified by some of the editors of Boswell's
Life of Johnson, because Wesley's name is not

actually mentioned. Johnson had been commending (rather dubiously) the preaching of the Methodists, and he went on to say that ' whatever might be thought of some Methodist teachers, he could scarcely doubt the sincerity of that man, who travelled nine hundred miles in a month, and preached twelve times a week ; for no adequate reward, merely temporal, could be given for such indefatigable labour '. Charles Wesley also appears to have been on terms of something like intimacy with Dr. Johnson. Thomas Jackson, Charles Wesley's biographer, found among his papers the following letter : ' Sir, I beg that you, and Mrs. and Miss Wesley, will dine with your brother and Mrs. Hall, at my house in Bolt Court, Fleet Street, to-morrow. That I have not sent sooner, if you knew the disordered state of my health, you would easily forgive me. I am, Sir, Your most humble Servant, Sam. Johnson.' This is not dated, but it must have been in or after the year 1776, since it was from that year to the end of his life that Johnson lived in Bolt Court. The Mrs. Hall mentioned in the letter is Wesley's sister Patty, with whom Johnson was especially friendly. He wished her to become an inmate of his house, and she would have done so if she had not feared the jealousy of Mrs. Williams and Mrs. Desmoulins, who were already established there. Boswell describes her in one place as ' lean, lank, preaching Mrs. Hall ', and in another as ' the sister of the Reverend Mr. John Wesley, and resembling him, as I thought, both in figure and in manner'. Other people remarked that Mrs. Hall was the most like her brother John of all the family, and Dr. Adam Clarke said that if they had been dressed alike he could not have distinguished the one from the other. On one occasion at least she got in a home thrust at Johnson. They had

HM

been talking of the unhappiness of human life, and she said, 'Doctor, you have always lived among the wits, not the saints ; and they are a race of people the most unlikely to seek true happiness, or find the pearl without price'.

Now, Dr. Johnson was undeniably a religious man. But his religious experience was decidedly not of the type which we find in the New Testament. It was penetrated throughout by fear and gloom, and there is not a trace of that glad assurance of the pardon and the peace of God which is characteristic of evangelical religion. All his life long Johnson (who was emphatically a man of courage) went in fear of death, or, rather, of what comes after death. Mrs. Knowles, the Quakeress, said to Boswell, who had spoken of his horror at the thought of death, 'Nay, thou shouldst not have a horror for what is the gate of life'. Whereupon Johnson remarked, with a gloomy air, 'No rational man can die without uneasy apprehension'. Mrs. Knowles said, 'The Scriptures tell us, *The righteous shall have hope in his death*'. 'Yes, madam, that is, he shall not have despair. But, consider, his hope of salvation must be founded on the terms on which it is promised that the mediation of our Saviour shall be applied to us – namely, obedience ; and where obedience has failed, then, as suppletory to it, repentance. But what man can say that his obedience has been such as he would approve of in another, or even in himself upon close examination, or that his repentance has not been such as to require being repented of ? No man can be sure that his obedience and repentance will obtain salvation.' Mrs. Knowles said, 'But divine intimation of acceptance may be made to the soul'. 'Madam, it may,' said Johnson, 'but I should not think the better of a man who should tell me on

his deathbed he was sure of salvation. A man
cannot be sure himself that he has divine intimation
of acceptance ; much less can he make others sure
that he has it.' Mrs. Knowles said, ' Does not St.
Paul say, *I have fought the good fight, I have finished my
course, henceforth there is laid up for me a crown of
righteousness ?*' ' Yes, madam,' said Johnson, ' but
here was a man inspired, a man who had been converted by supernatural interposition.' It was
immediately after this last conversation, by the
way, that Johnson went on to speak of John Wesley,
and said, ' He can talk well on any subject '. It
looks as if the mention by Mrs. Knowles of spiritual
assurance had led on in Johnson's mind to the
thought of Wesley, whose doctrine centred so much
around that experience.

Johnson once told Boswell that ' he never had a
moment in which death was not terrible to him '.
Boswell adds for himself, on the occasion of one of
these conversations about death and judgement
and the consolations of religion, ' I thought that
the gloom of uncertainty in solemn religious speculation, being mingled with hope, was yet more
consolatory than the emptiness of infidelity. A
man can live in thick air, but perishes in an ex-
hausted receiver '. On another occasion Johnson
said, ' As I cannot be *sure* that I have fulfilled the
conditions on which salvation is granted, I am
afraid I may be one of those who shall be damned '.
Boswell, in spite of Johnson's uttering this ' passionately and loudly ', ventured to say, ' But may not
a man attain to such a degree of hope as not to be
uneasy from the fear of death ? ' ' A man may
have such a degree of hope', said Johnson, 'as to
keep him quiet. You see I am not quiet, from the
vehemence with which I talk ; but I do not
despair.' Here Mrs. Adams said, ' You seem, sir,

to forget the merits of our Redeemer'. Johnson answered, ' Madam, I do not forget the merits of my Redeemer ; but my Redeemer has said that He will set some on His right hand and some on His left '. Then, ' in gloomy agitation ', he exclaimed, ' I'll have no more on't ! '

On still another occasion Boswell rather quaintly records that he stated to Johnson ' an anxious thought by which a sincere Christian might be disturbed, even when conscious of having lived a good life, so far as is consistent with human infirmity ; he might fear that he should afterward fall away, and be guilty of such crimes as would render all his former religion vain. Could there be, upon this awful subject, such a thing as balancing of accounts ? Suppose a man who has led a good life for seven years, commits an act of wickedness, and instantly dies ; will his former good life have any effect in his favour ? ' Johnson said, ' Sir, if a man has led a good life for seven years, and then is hurried by passion to do what is wrong, and is suddenly carried off, depend upon it he will have the reward of his seven years' good life ; God will not take a catch of him '.

The whole assumption in these conversations is that of a sort of moralistic Deism. There is a God, and He is the Judge of men. If a man lives a good life he will be rewarded and saved ; if he lives a bad life he will be punished and lost. If there is some question as to the balance of good and evil in his life, we may hope that the Judge will not be too strict and severe. That is all ; there is no thought of God as the heavenly Father, with a Father's pity and a Father's love ; no thought of the Son of God as the Friend of sinners, who died, the righteous for the unrighteous, to bring us to God. There is no sense of our entire unworthiness, at the best, as

well as at the worst ; no realization of the faith
which is the gift of God, and which enables us
to lay hold of God and of the life which is life
eternal.   The whole range of thought, in fact, is
sub-Christian.

Now, when all allowance has been made for Dr.
Johnson's disposition toward melancholy (on which
one sometimes imagines he almost prided himself),
all this is more than personally significant.   For his
conception of religion was the current one, and it
was a kind of legalism at the best.   He had never
really understood the wonder of the grace of God.
For him, and for the average churchman in the
middle of the eighteenth century, salvation was the
reward of obedience to the law of God ;   that is
to say, the recompense of a meritorious life, with
the saving clause that what was lacking in obedience
might be made up by repentance.   As a man could
never be sure that either his obedience or his
penitence was sufficient, he could never be sure of
salvation.   Salvation was something earned by
obedience, or, in defect of that, by repentance ;   it
was not something freely given to undeserving
sinners by the unspeakable mercy of God.   But if
the gospel means anything at all, it surely means
that.   The whole system that revolves around the
thought of morality and merit passes out of sight
when the soul of the penitent sinner is dealing with
the Saviour who loved us and gave Himself for us,
and a man is saved from his sins simply and solely
because he casts himself upon the unmerited mercy
of God in Christ, whatever his merits or his de-
merits may have been.   When he has found that
undeserved mercy, he rejoices in it with an unspeakable joy, and then he serves God gladly,
without any thought of merit, in the past or in the
future.   But the whole of this evangelical experience

was a sealed book to Dr. Johnson. All that witnessed of it in the New Testament was ruled out as
exceptional and miraculous. The Apostles might
have an experience of assurance, for they were
inspired men and there was a supernatural element
in their lives, but for an ordinary man in the
eighteenth century to pretend to any such experience was mere presumption. In all this Dr. Johnson
was thoroughly representative of his century.[1]

It was this type of religion, that consists, at the
worst, in moral conduct and an observance of the
rites of the Church, or, at the best, in these things
with the addition of prayer, penitence, mortification, and a spirit of fear – it was this which Wesley
was encountering and exposing all his days, with
his lips and with his pen. He understood it thoroughly, for it had once been his own notion of
religion. He writes in *An Earnest Appeal to Men of
Reason and Religion* : ' We see, on every side, either
men of no religion at all, or of a lifeless, formal
religion. We are grieved at the sight ; and should
greatly rejoice, if by any means we might convince
some that there is a better religion to be attained –
a religion worthy of God that gave it. And this we
conceive to be none other than love ; the love of
God and of all mankind ; the loving God with all

---

[1] Warburton, the Bishop of Gloucester, in his work *On the Office and
Operations of the Holy Spirit*, argues at length that the Spirit of God inspired
the Apostles for the purpose of writing the New Testament, and that then
the work of the Spirit was practically done. ' Thus the promise of our
blessed Master, that the Comforter should abide with us for ever, has been
eminently fulfilled. For though, according to the promise, *His ordinary
influence occasionally assists the faithful of all ages, yet His constant abode and
supreme illumination is in the sacred Scriptures of the New Testament*. . . . When the
rule of faith was perfected in an authentic collection of the Apostolic
writings, part of His office was transferred upon the sacred canon, and *His
enlightening grace was not to be expected in so abundant effusion*.' As Miss Julia
Wedgwood acutely remarked, we can judge the spirit of Hanoverian
theology by the simple fact that Warburton's reasoning did not seem
extraordinary to his age – ' except the Methodists, none of his contemporaries thought it monstrous '. – *John Wesley and the Evangelical Reaction of the
Eighteenth Century*, p. 327.

our heart, and soul, and strength, as having first loved us, as the Fountain of all the good we have received, and of all we ever hope to enjoy ; and the loving every soul which God hath made, every man on earth, as our own soul. . . . This religion we have been following after for many years, as many know, if they would testify.   But all this time, seeking wisdom, we found it not ; we were spending our strength in vain.   And now, being under full conviction of this, we declare it to all mankind, for we desire not that others should wander out of the way as we have done before them ; but rather that they may profit by our loss, that they may go (though we did not, having then no man to guide us) the straight way to the religion of love, even by faith. Now faith (supposing the Scripture to be of God) is πραγμάτων ἔλεγχος οὐ βλεπομένων, the demonstrative evidence of things not seen, the supernatural evidence of things invisible, not perceived by eyes of flesh, or by any of our natural senses and faculties. Faith is that divine evidence whereby the spiritual man discerneth God, and the things of God.   It is with regard to the spiritual world, what sense is with regard to the natural world.   It is the spiritual sensation of every soul that is born of God.'[1]   He states again, in *A Farther Appeal to Men of Reason and Religion*, that it was many years after he was ordained before he became convinced of the great evangelical truths which afterwards were the principal message of Methodism.   ' During all that time I was utterly ignorant of the nature and condition of justification.   Sometimes I confounded it with sanctification (particularly when I was in Georgia) ; at other times I had some confused notion about the forgiveness of sins ; but then I took it for granted the time of this must be either the hour of

[1] Wesley's *Works*, VIII, pp. 3–4.

death, or the day of judgement. I was equally ignorant of the nature of saving faith, apprehending it to mean no more than " a firm assent to all the propositions contained in the Old and New Testaments ".[1]

The lack of evangelical insight of which Wesley writes appears again and again, in all sorts of people, at the period. It is reflected in the literature of the time, as well as constantly referred to in Wesley's own writings. In a letter to Dr. Robertson, written in September 1753, Wesley makes some remarks on Ramsay's *Principles of Religion*. He quotes the statement, ' The immediate, essential, necessary means of reuniting men to God are prayer, mortification, and self-denial ', and comments, ' No : the immediate, essential, necessary means of reuniting men to God is living faith, and that alone. Without this, I cannot be reunited to God ; with this, I cannot but be reunited. Prayer, mortification, and self-denial, are the fruits of faith, and the grand means of continuing and increasing it '.

The central elements in the Christian experience were thus denied, debased, or ignored. The life of self-renunciation was not one of sacrificial joy, lived in the strength and for the sake of Christ, in thankfulness and devotion to Him ; it was a penitential sentence endured in the hope of winning the forgiveness of sins at the last. Faith was not a heartfelt trust in Christ : it was an assent to the truth of the Scriptures and the creed of the Church. Assurance was not the privilege of every believer, and if express passages of the New Testament were cited on the issue, the reply was at once that such things were miraculous, and though given to the Apostles, were not to be expected by any one to-day. If any man claimed an experience of assurance, that was

---

[1] Wesley's *Works*, VIII, p. 111.

merely proof of presumption on his part, for it was
pretending to special gifts and special revelations.
This, once more, might be repeatedly illustrated
from the actual words and events of the time.
Wesley wrote in his *Journal* under the date of
June 25, 1745, when a Methodist had actually been
thrown into prison on account of his religion, ' I
asked a little gentleman at St. Just what objection
there was to Edward Greenfield. He said, " Why,
the man is well enough in other things ; but his
impudence the gentlemen cannot bear. Why, sir,
he says he knows his sins are forgiven ! " ' Bishop
Butler, the greatest Christian thinker of the age,
was much of the same mind as the ' little gentleman ' at St. Just. When Wesley was at Bristol in
1739, and had an interview with him, after saying
that ' men were justified on account of some moral
goodness in them ', and that ' faith itself is a good
work ; it is a virtuous temper of mind ', Butler
went on to say, ' Sir, the pretending to extraordinary
revelations and gifts of the Holy Ghost is a horrid
thing – a very horrid thing ! ' No wonder the
bishop finally said, ' You have no business here ;
you are not commissioned to preach in this diocese.
Therefore I advise you to go hence '.

   It is pathetic to remember that when Bishop
Butler was dying he said to his chaplain, ' Though
I have endeavoured to avoid sin, and to please God
to the utmost of my power, yet from consciousness
of perpetual infirmities, I am still afraid to die '.
The chaplain said, ' My Lord, you have forgotten
that Jesus Christ is a Saviour '. ' True,' said Butler,
' but how shall I know that He is a Saviour for
me ? ' ' My Lord,' the chaplain said, ' it is written,
Him that cometh unto Me I will in no wise cast out.'
' True,' said the dying prelate, ' and I am surprised
that though I have read that scripture I suppose a

thousand times over, I never felt its virtue till this
moment. And now I die happy.'

It has been shrewdly remarked that in the *Analogy*
Butler used almost every type of argument that can
be used in favour of religion, except the argument
from experience. It was, of course, the central element in religious experience – the living faith which
is the gift of God – that Butler did not understand,
for all his wisdom and all his goodness. Alike to
the mind of Butler and of Johnson, and of almost
every one else at that period, it was a piece of
daring presumption for any man to believe (in the
language of the Apostle) that the Spirit of God
bears witness with our spirit that we are children
of God.

An actual *experience* of redeeming grace, in fact,
was not regarded as a thing to be expected : there
ought to be a moral life, and a sincere assent to the
creed of the Church, and some repentance, since
every man has sinned, and there might be some
hope of salvation through the mercy of God, if the
life had been sufficiently virtuous, and that was all.
There was not to be looked for, except in the first
age of the Church, which was an age of miracles,
an actual work and witness of God in the soul,
which became an inward experience of the believer.
To use the language of the New Testament of
one's own soul, to claim the Apostle's experience
of the pardon and peace of God as one's own heritage – this was merely spiritual presumption and
pride.

To put it in a word, Methodism recovered and
restored to the fellowship of believers the evangelical
experience as a reality in the soul and in the life.
The salvation of the soul is not an exalted hope or a
distant possibility : it is a present fact. It is not, as
Wesley wrote, merely ' the soul's going to heaven,

eternal happiness. . . . It is not a blessing which lies on the other side death, or as we usually speak, in the other world. . . . It is not something at a distance : it is a present thing ; a blessing which, through the free mercy of God we are now in possession of '.[1] He wrote again, in *A Farther Appeal to Men of Reason and Religion* : ' By salvation I mean, not barely, according to the vulgar notion, deliverance from hell, or going to heaven ; but a present deliverance from sin, a restoration of the soul to its primitive health, its original purity ; a recovery of the divine nature ; the renewal of our souls after the image of God, in righteousness and true holiness, in justice, mercy, and truth.'[2]

Methodism has often been criticized on the double ground that it is far too subjective and far too individualist.   There is clearly a close relation between the one charge and the other, and it is perhaps natural that such criticisms should be made from outside, because of the stress that has always been placed by Methodists upon a personal experience of religion.   Pusey once said that Methodism stood for ' justification by feeling '.   Nothing could be more false.   From the days of Wesley down to the present, no Methodist has ever dreamed of grounding the forgiveness of sins upon anything but the free grace of God and the redemptive work of Christ.   But if a penitent soul is restored to the favour of God by a humble trust in the merits of the Redeemer, may he not be assured of it by the Spirit of God ?   And how is he to be assured of it except by a spiritual consciousness, an awareness of the mercy of God in his soul which he can hardly describe otherwise than by saying that he feels it within himself ?   As Wesley himself wrote immediately

[1] Wesley's *Works*, VI, p. 44.
[2] Wesley's *Works*, VIII, p. 47.

before the account which he gives of his experience on May 24, 1738 : ' Besides, I saw well, no one could, in the nature of things, have such a sense of forgiveness and not *feel* it.' There is, of course, an ambiguity in the word ' feeling ', which has entered into some criticisms of Methodism much as the similar ambiguity of *Gefühl* has entered into some criticisms of Schleiermacher. ' Feeling ' may or may not have a connotation of emotionalism. It may mean merely a sense of something, an immediate awareness of it, or it may mean that and, in addition, a stirring of the emotions so deep that the emotional significance of the word prevails over everything else. Now in an experience of conversion or an experience of assurance there may be strong emotional excitement, or there may not. But Methodists have never really stressed the emotional side as anything in the nature of a proof of spiritual facts or spiritual conditions. They have always meant, at any rate, to stress the fact of a spiritual awareness, a spiritual certainty, which may or may not have a strongly marked emotional accompaniment.

Again, Methodism has been accused, more than once, of being too individualist. Troeltsch once called Methodism ' the renewal of orthodox Christianity in a quite individualistic accentuated form '.[1] The emphasis is correct so far as it is positive, but the negative implication is utterly wrong. Methodism did insist upon an intensely individual experience, and rightly : the last reality of religion must be an individual experience, for the simple reason that men are individuals.[2] But Methodism was

[1] *The Social Teaching of the Christian Churches*, II, p. 721.
[2] ' Experience means consciousness, and consciousness can only be real in individuals, and the appeal to experience means, of course, an appeal to a consciousness of God which individuals enjoy. But not only was the individual's apprehension of God to be tested in fellowship and verified by

never merely individualistic. There was always from the beginning a heavy stress on the fact of fellowship. The whole constitution of Methodism as a community has always depended on fellowship in its most genuine and intimate form. Henry Moore says that in 1729 Wesley went many miles to ask the counsel of ' a serious man ',[1] who said, ' Sir, you wish to serve God and go to heaven ? Remember that you cannot serve Him alone. You must therefore find companions or make them ; the Bible knows nothing of solitary religion '.[2] Wesley never forgot that counsel, and the Methodist community was organized almost from the first in small groups where fellowship could be of the most intimate kind. There has probably never been, in the whole history of the Church of Christ, any community where religious fellowship was quite so real or so deep as it has been in Methodism, and, in the face of such a fact, to accuse the movement of excessive individualism seems a little queer.

But the fellowship was based upon a shared experience of religion. It was a fellowship of those who had found redemption in Christ, and the bond of union was a common faith and a common experience. Experience, indeed, is the governing principle with Methodism all the way through, not only with respect to the actualities of personal

the moral conduct of daily life. Their experience was based on the objective facts of an historical revelation. There were three stages in the process of revelation, in the Christian sense of the word, if we may analyse what is implicit in their own accounts. First, there is one historical figure, the Perfect Revelation of God, Jesus in His Life and Death. Secondly, there is Revelation in the continuation of the work of Jesus, in the religious consciousness of the primitive Church, the experience which the New Testament calls the Spirit. And thirdly, there is the Revelation as it is appropriated and made real and vivid in the daily consciousness of the individual Methodist himself, in mind and heart and conscience.' – R. N. Flew, *The Idea of Perfection in Christian Theology*, pp. 316–17.

[1] Probably the Rev. Mr. Hoole, the Rector of Haxey.

[2] *Life of Wesley*, I, p. 162.

religion, but with regard to religious rites, and ecclesiastical regulations, and evangelistic methods, and indeed everything else. Wesley's one concern was, in effect, as to whether the thing in question, whatever it might be, proved itself, in actual experience, to be useful and effective. If it did that, as a matter of attested fact, then he troubled no more as to whether it had the sanction of antiquity or not, whether the ecclesiastical authorities approved it or not, whether he himself liked it or not, as a matter of personal taste.

Wesley's pragmatic methods are in evidence all through his life. He began with an ample stock of ecclesiastical and theological prejudices, and one by one he discarded them under the pressure of religious facts. At one time, as he says, he would have ' thought the saving of souls almost a sin if it had not been done in a church ', but Whitefield had been compelled to preach out of doors, and Wesley saw the results. He could not doubt that spiritual good was done, and that the blessing of God was upon the work. So, early in April 1739, he began to preach in the open air at Bristol. The day before at ' a little Society ' in Nicholas Street he had expounded the Sermon on the Mount, which is, as he drily remarks, ' one pretty remarkable precedent of field-preaching '.

At one time Wesley had the most violent objection to laymen preaching, and when Thomas Maxfield began to exhort he hurried back to London to stop him. Fortunately he saw his mother before he saw Maxfield, and that wise woman said, ' John, take care what you do with respect to that young man, for he is as surely called of God to preach as you are. Examine what have been the fruits of his preaching, and hear him yourself '. Wesley found that many had been brought to repentance and faith through the preaching of Maxfield, and that was enough. Henceforth Wesley had no scruples on the subject. He began to employ laymen as preachers of the gospel, and set hundreds of them to work in that way during the years that followed. So it was throughout his life. He was always convinced by the logic of facts, and by the witness of experience.

This is entirely characteristic. The whole genius of early Methodism was experimental. It was not a question of anything abstract, or doctrinaire, or traditional : it was a question of matter of fact in the religious life and the spiritual experience of men : of things really experienced in the soul, and witnessed in the life. In early Methodism the Acts of the Apostles came to life again. The lives of sinful men were suddenly, startlingly, miraculously changed ; those who had sought to serve God in a spirit of fear, and had spent years in spiritual bondage, found a glad assurance of the abundant pardon of God and the peace that passeth understanding. These things happened, and what had come to pass in the unseen life of the souls of men was manifested and proved by the change in their outward life. John Wesley had shared this experience himself : he witnessed the effects of it in the lives of unnumbered other men. 'The whole question turns chiefly, if not wholly, on matter of fact ' . . . ' I do and will testify the things I have both seen and heard. . . .' This was the note that Methodism sounded from the first, and will sound, I hope, throughout all the days to come.

The religious contribution of Methodism was, therefore, the recovery of the evangelical witness and the evangelical experience – the spiritual fact that real penitence, real faith, a real surrender of the heart and life to Christ, brings an assurance of the pardon and the peace of God, from which a sense of wonder and joy naturally spring, and which leads directly to an intimacy of religious fellowship and a zeal of passionate evangelism.

CHAPTER V

THE THEOLOGICAL CONTRIBUTION

I<small>T</small> has often been said that the contribution of
Methodism to theology is negligible, but that judgement is a very superficial one.   It is true, of course,
that John Wesley was not a formal theologian,
and that he did not leave behind him a massive
compendium of doctrine to rank among the
theological classics.   It should be remembered,
however, that Wesley's *Sermons* and his *Notes on the
New Testament* have admirably served the purpose of
doctrinal standards in Methodism for six generations
past.   The *Sermons* are distinguished by a real and
remarkable insight into theological issues in their
relation to religious experience,[1] and the *Notes on
the New Testament* (which are largely indebted to
Bengel, the greatest New Testament scholar of that
age) present as sound an exposition as is to be found
in the eighteenth century, as well as an amended
text which is really a very remarkable anticipation
of the Revised Version of a hundred and thirty years
later.   But though no one would claim that Wesley
is to be reckoned among the more famous theologians of the universal Church, and though he neither
attempted nor desired to make any doctrinal innova-
tions, it is nevertheless a fact that Methodism

---

[1] It may be noted that Dr. Friedrich Loofs, one of the most eminent
historians of dogma, writes with great respect of Wesley's sermons.   He
remarks upon the wealth of their content, and the orderly progress of
thought, the practical earnestness, and the sheer lucidity which characterize
them all. – ' Methodismus ', in Herzog-Hauck, *Realencyklopädie*, Heft 119,
p. 767.

accomplished a theological revolution, and that in more than one direction.

It has been remarked by Loofs, with real discernment, that the interest of Methodism in theology is confined mainly to the *loci salutares*.[1] Neither Wesley at the beginning, nor the representative theologians of Methodism since, have had much concern with the mere scholasticism of theology ; and I do not think they need any defence at that point. Doubtless such intellectual refinements will always attract the thinker, but the religious value of a doctrine lessens as the philosophical interest increases, and in theological subtleties it is the philosophical interest that necessarily prevails. This does not mean that a theological positivism like that of Ritschl is justified in its exclusiveness, for there will always be metaphysical facts and factors which are implied in the most simple and the most practical version of religion, and, since the intellect has its rights, these abstract speculations will be pursued, and, indeed, ought to be pursued. But the fact remains that the vital things in religion are not, first of all, intellectual issues, and a great evangelical revival like Methodism was naturally concerned, in the first place, with the redemptive facts and the redemptive experiences. The stress has always been, in Methodist theology, upon the redeeming love of God in Christ, and the work of the Holy Spirit ; upon repentance, and faith, and conversion, and fellowship, and holiness.   That

[1] Die weiteren Kürzungen der 39 Artikel durch J. Wesley werden aus seiner Scheu vor unnötiger Breite und aus der bewussten Absicht, nicht Nebensächliches (wie *art.* 3 *anglic. de descensu Christi*) mit Hauptsächlichem zu mischen, zu erklären sein. Beides einte sich in seinem Bestreben, den Menschen das Evangelium in seiner schlichten Grösse so nahe zu bringen, dass es sich an ihren Gewissen bewähren könne. Und diese Tendenz zu einer Beschränkung auf die *loci salutares*, dies Intesesse an der christlichen Erfahrung und ihrem Zeugnis für den Glauben, es ist noch heute ein Vorzug methodistischer Theologie. – ' Methodismus ', in Herzog-Hauck, *Realencyklopädie*, Heft 119, p. 800.

practical concern with the salvation of men is really
the governing factor in all that can be said about the
relation of Methodism to theology, for it lies behind
each of the three special contributions that Methodism may claim to have made to modern theological thought and method. It is this which explains
alike the characteristic stand upon experience, in
which Methodism anticipated Schleiermacher; and
the victorious attack upon Calvinism; and the
emphasis upon sanctification. It was because the
early Methodists were primarily concerned with
the salvation of men that they came to stress the
fact of a personal experience and a personal
certainty of redemption. It was for the same reason
that they passionately opposed a doctrine which
denied salvation to the larger part of mankind. It
was for the same reason, again, that they emphasized
the fact and explored the nature of holiness, since
that is both the unfailing result and the undeniable
evidence of a real and personal experience of
salvation.

I

First of all, then, Wesley and the early Methodists
grounded religion and theology in the fact of experience. This was a revolution in theological practice,
for it was the revolutionary application to theology
of what is really scientific method. At the Reformation, Catholicism took its final stand on the
authority of the Church, and Protestantism took its
first stand on the authority of the Bible. Methodism, without altogether realizing what it was doing,
shifted the ultimate authority in religion to the last
place and the right place – to religious experience.
The early *Minutes of Conference* are enough to
illustrate this. They consist largely of a careful

examination of the experiences of the spiritual life ;
one might almost say of a systematic analysis of
religious experience. It is sometimes suggested that
religion of the evangelical and experimental type
is merely individualist. It is, in a way, as all real
religion must be, for no man can repent or believe
or yield up his life to God except for himself. At
the very heart of it religion must be intensely
individualist. But it must be remembered that
the individual experience never stands by itself.
Behind it there is always the correspondent and
corroborative experience of the community of the
redeemed.[1] Along with the emphasis on personal
religion in early Methodism there always went the
stress on religious fellowship. The experience which
was so primary in Methodism was the experience
of the individual soul, but it was more than that –
it was the experience of many separate souls, united
in a community of believers. And the experience
of the community was behind the experience of the
individual, as much as the experience of the individual was behind the experience of the community.

It is significant that Wesley was constantly col-
lecting from his preachers and his people detailed
accounts of their religious experience. This was
really the origin of that astonishing collection of
autobiographies, *The Lives of the Early Methodist
Preachers*. When we read them to-day we are
attracted by their wonderful style, and the amazing
wealth of romantic detail they contain, but Wesley's
purpose in asking his preachers to write an account
of their lives was really to secure a full history of
their religious experience.

---

[1] It has been well remarked, as a very significant fact, that ' Methodist
doctrine is the direct result of collective deliberation, based upon testimony
and discussion in the Societies, tested and thought out by the leaders and by
Wesley himself '. – Sydney G. Dimond, *The Psychology of the Methodist
Revival*, p. 214.

It is a casual illustration of this attitude of mind, again, that Wesley made it a matter of inquiry as to whether there was anything in religious experience that confirmed the doctrine of the Trinity, and concluded that, while the whole mystery lies in the manner of the Triunity, there is no doubt as to the fact, because ' the knowledge of the Three-One God is interwoven with all true Christian faith, with all vital religion. . . . I know not how any one can be a Christian believer until he hath, as St. John speaks, " the witness in himself " ; till " the Spirit of God witnesses with his spirit that he is a child of God " ; that is, in effect, till God the Holy Ghost witnesses that God the Father has accepted him through the merits of God the Son ; and, having this witness, he honours the Son, and the blessed Spirit, " even as he honours the Father ". Not that every Christian believer *adverts* to this ; perhaps, at first, not one in twenty. But if you ask any of them a few questions, you will easily find it implied in what he believes '.[1]

These are more or less incidental illustrations of Wesley's method. What is more important is that all the way through, in dealing with personal religion, he was not content with anything less than the reality of experience. He urged this upon all those whom he addressed. He never wearied of warning men that ' everything else, whether negative or external, is utterly wide of the mark ',[2] that religion does not consist in mere forms, or mere morality, or mere orthodoxy, but in an experience of redemption wrought in ' men's hearts and lives '.[3] In one place, when he is expressly pleading with formal Christians, he writes : ' Do you go further yet ? Do you add to the doing no harm, the

[1] Wesley's *Works*, VI, p. 205.   [2] Wesley's *Works*, V, p. 38.
[3] Wesley's *Works*, VI, p. 276.

attending all the ordinances of God ?   Do you, at
all opportunities, partake of the Lord's Supper, use
public and private prayer ? fast often ? hear and
search the Scriptures, and meditate thereon ?
These things, likewise, ought you to have done,
from the time you first set your face toward heaven.
Yet these things are nothing, being alone.   They
are nothing without " the weightier matters of the
law ".   And those you have forgotten ;   at least,
you *experience* them not – faith, mercy, and the love
of God : holiness of heart : heaven opened in the
soul.'[1]

One might go through Wesley's writings and
quote illustrations of this attitude endlessly.   It
appears even before his evangelical conversion.   In
the preface of his edition of the *Imitatio Christi*,
which was published in 1735, Wesley writes : ' If
there be any who searches for the understanding of
divine truths in the path of obedience and experience, who carefully observes the kingdom of God,
and the workings of the Holy Spirit in his own soul,
and who continually endeavours after an entire
conformity to the life of his great Master : they
may hope, by the blessing of God on this treatise,
to attain to a more full and inward knowledge of
Christ. . . . The great practical truths of religion,
the mysteries of the inward kingdom of God, cannot
be fully discerned, but by those readers who have
read the same thing in their own souls.   These
cannot be clearly known, but by those who derive
their knowledge, " not from commentaries, but
experience ", who by living the life of Christ, by
treading in His steps, and suffering the will of God
to rule in them as it did in Him, have attained to
what the heart of a natural man cannot conceive –
the knowing of God as they ought to know.   This

[1] Wesley's *Works*, V, p. 430.

is that *inward, practical, experimental, feeling knowledge,* so frequently commended by our author.'[1]

Three years later, still before (though immediately before) the great experience of May 24, 1738, when he was arguing with Peter Böhler, Wesley demanded that the dispute should be put ' upon the issue which I desired, namely, Scripture and *experience* '. More than forty years later he associates Scripture and experience in exactly the same way. He writes : ' *Experience* is sufficient to confirm a doctrine which is grounded on Scripture : though many fancy they experience what they do not, this is no prejudice to real experience.'[2] Wesley never dreamt, of course, of pitting the Word of God and the experience of believers one against the other ; he believed that they must agree, if the experience was genuine, and if the Scripture was rightly understood. The appeal to experience was in that day a novel method, but there was no novel result in doctrine. As a matter of fact, the Methodists have always been, and are to-day, steadily orthodox as a community. The great religious facts and the great theological doctrines were unchallenged, but Wesley and the early Methodists, without in the least doubting the real inspiration of the Scriptures or the corporate authority of the Church, looked to the facts of religious experience rather than to a Scriptural or an ecclesiastical warrant for the final proof of spiritual realities. Methodism, in the words of Dr. Maximin Piette, ' jette un pont entre le conservatisme orthodoxe et le pragmatisme subjectiviste '.[3]

[1] Wesley's *Works*, XIV, p. 223.

[2] Wesley's *Works*, V, p. 133.

[3] Au point de vue doctrinal, le méthodisme occupe une situation unique par la primauté qu'il accorde à l'expérience religieuse. Réaction contre l'antinomisme luthérien, réaction contre le calvinisme aux décrets absolus, réalisation du libre examen dans les limites d'une forte organisation

There is no mistaking the fact that, with Wesley, experience is always the final test, though he probably did not always realize that it was so. On almost every page of his writings there is the appeal to experience, explicitly or implicitly made. It would be wearisome, even if it were possible, to quote even a representative series of utterances on this point. Here are a few. ' How clearly does this [i.e. the necessity of the moral law] agree with the *experience* of every true believer ! '[1] ' How does *experience* confirm this ! . . . It is matter of daily *experience* that by grace are we thus saved through faith.'[2] ' We believe there is [a direct testimony of the Holy Spirit in the believing soul] . . . because this plain meaning of the word of God is confirmed by the *experience* of innumerable children of God.'[3] ' Faith alone it is which effectually answers this end [the fulfilment of the law of righteousness in our hearts and lives] as we learn from daily *experience*.'[4]

Perhaps the most striking passage in Wesley's writings along this line is in *A Letter to the Reverend Dr. Conyers Middleton*, where he says : ' If it were possible (which I conceive it is not) to shake the traditional evidence of Christianity, still he that hath the internal evidence (and every true believer hath the witness or evidence in himself) would stand firm and unshaken. Still he could say to those who were striking at the external evidence, "Beat on the sack of Anaxagoras". But you can no more hurt my evidence of Christianity than the tyrant could hurt the spirit of that wise man. I

---

disciplinaire, acheminement de la théologie vers les théories de Schleiermacher et de William James : telles sont ses notes caractéristiques. Il jette un pont entre le conservatisme orthodoxe et le pragmatisme subjectiviste. – *La Réaction Wesléyenne dans l'Évolution Protestante*, p. ix. (But the reference to Lutheran Antinomianism is, of course, a piece of pure Catholic prejudice.)

[1] Wesley's *Works*, V, p. 444.   [3] Wesley's *Works*, V, p. 132.
[2] Wesley's *Works*, V, pp. 362-3.   [4] Wesley's *Works*, V, p. 464.

have sometimes been almost inclined to believe, that the wisdom of God has, in most later ages, permitted the external evidence of Christianity to be more or less clogged and incumbered for this very end, that men (of reflection especially) might not altogether rest there, but be constrained to look into themselves also, and attend to the light shining in their hearts. Nay, it seems (if it may be allowed for us to pry so far into the reasons of the divine dispensations) that, particularly in this age, God suffers all kinds of objections to be raised against the traditional evidence of Christianity, that men of understanding, though unwilling to give it up, yet, at the same time they defend this evidence, may not rest the whole strength of their cause thereon, but seek a deeper and firmer support for it. Without this I cannot but doubt, whether they can long maintain their cause ; whether, if they do not obey the loud call of God, and lay far more stress than they have hitherto done on the internal evidence of Christianity, they will not, one after another, give up the external, and (in heart at least) go over to those whom they are now contending with ; so that in a century or two the people of England will be fairly divided into real Deists and real Christians.'[1] This is almost prophetic in its insight into what was deficient in eighteenth-century apologetics, and in its sense of the changed approach and the changed defence of the future, but the point to remark at the moment is the plain realization in these words that the real and final evidence of religion is to be found in religious experience.

The spiritual certainty that belongs to the reality of religious experience was generally described by Wesley and the early Methodists in the Pauline term, 'the witness of the Spirit'. The Apostle writes

[1] Wesley's *Works*, X, pp. 76–7.

in Romans viii. 16, ' The Spirit itself beareth witness with our spirit that we are the children of God ', and Wesley's interpretation of the passage seems the only possible one – that as there is a witness of our own spirit, which assures us of our own sincerity, so that we can no longer doubt that we have really repented and believed and cast ourselves upon the mercy of God in Christ, there is also a witness of the Holy Spirit which assures us of the grace of God, so that we can no longer doubt that we are the children of God. It is only holiness of life that can prove to others that we are the children of God, but it is only the testimony of God Himself through His Spirit that can prove to ourselves that we are the children of God. How else could any man know it ?

This express point, which is the very crux of the Methodist faith and the Methodist witness, is dealt with by the Wesleys again and again. In one of the sermons John Wesley writes : ' How can any man *know* that he is alive to God ? Even as you know that your body is now alive. Faith is the life of the soul ; and if ye have this life abiding in you, ye want no marks to evidence it *to yourself*, but ἔλεγχος πνεύματος, that divine consciousness, that *witness* of God, which is more and greater than ten thousand human witnesses.'[1] In another sermon he writes : ' I would ask him, then, that proposes this question [i.e. how it appears to us that we are the children of God], How does it appear to you, that you are alive ? And that you are now in ease, and not in pain ? Are you not immediately conscious of it ? By the same *immediate consciousness*, you will know if your soul is alive to God ; if you are saved from the pain of proud wrath, and have the ease of a meek and quiet spirit. By the same

---

[1] Wesley's *Works*, V, p. 28.

means you cannot but perceive if you love, rejoice, and delight in God.'[1]

The same general meaning is given to saving faith as to the more precise conception of the witness of the Spirit. That, again, is an inward evidence, an inward conviction, imparted to the soul by the Spirit of God. Wesley writes : ' Faith, in general, is defined by the Apostle πραγμάτων ἔλεγχος οὐ βλεπομένων, *an evidence*, a divine *evidence and conviction* (the word means both) *of things not seen* ; not visible, not perceivable, either by sight, or by any other of the external senses. It implies both a supernatural evidence of God, and of the things of God ; a kind of spiritual *light* exhibited to the soul, and a supernatural *sight* or perception thereof.'[2] And, in another sermon : ' Every one, therefore, who denies the existence of such a testimony [the witness of the Spirit] does in effect deny justification by faith. It follows, that either he never experienced this, either he never was justified, or that he has forgotten, as St. Peter speaks, τοῦ καθαρισμοῦ τῶν πάλαι αὐτου ἀμαρτιῶν, *the purification from his former sins* ; the *experience* he then had himself.'[3] The central argument of the sermon last quoted (that on ' The Witness of the Spirit ') is really that what is, on the part of God, through grace, a work and witness of the Holy Spirit, becomes on our side, through faith, a fact of experience, and that the whole confirmation of a truth taught in Scripture is by way of personal experience ; though the reality of that inward experience is always to be proved by a life of goodness.

The assurance which Wesley in earlier life had thought to be an invariable accompaniment of

[1] Wesley's *Works*, V, p. 114.

[2] Wesley's *Works*, VI, p. 46.

[3] Wesley's *Works*, V, p. 129.

saving faith, he came to see in later years (here, again, taught by the facts of experience) to be rather the privilege of all believers, and the posses- sion of many, but not of every one. He wrote to Professor Rutherforth in 1768 : ' I believe a consciousness of being in the favour of God (which I do not term *full assurance*, since it is frequently weakened, nay, perhaps interrupted, by returns of doubt and fear) is the common privilege of Chris- tians, fearing God and working righteousness. Yet I do not affirm there are no exceptions to this general rule. . . . Therefore I have not, for many years, thought a consciousness of acceptance to be essential to justifying faith.' But Wesley never wavered from the belief that an experience of assurance is the normal result of a real penitence, a real faith, and a real surrender to Christ – that it is the privilege, and that it ought to be the possession of every redeemed soul.

The vital position given to religious experience seems to be inevitable when the issues are really thought out. The whole truth and the whole existence of religion are bound up with it. Is it a fact that God makes Himself known to men ? Then that is the primary reality in religion, and there are two sides to it – the action of God upon the soul of man, and the experience in the soul of man which realizes the action of God. As in the general fact of existence there would never have been any universe apart from the creative act of God, and there would never have been any experience of the universe apart from the mind of man, so in the special fact of religion. Unless God makes Himself known to man, and unless man knows that God has made Himself known to man, there is no possibility of religion as a reality. The act of God on the higher side, the experience of man on the lower side, inseparably conjoined, because without the first there would be no possibility of the second, and without the second there could be no knowledge of the first – here is the primary fact of religion.   All else is secondary and resultant.   Both the Bible and the Church are the result of that religious experience which is the response to the action of God upon the soul of man.   If God had not revealed Himself to men, and men had not known it, the religious literature that we call the Bible, and the redeemed fellowship that we call the Church, would never have come into existence at all.

Now the importance of this new emphasis upon religious experience in early Methodism, as a matter of theological history, lies in the fact that it falls into place in the main line of development of human knowledge in modern times.   When Wesley and the early Methodists instinctively appealed to the Christian experience as the main proof of the Christian faith, they were only doing, almost unconsciously, what Schleiermacher did deliberately and definitely some generations later, but their action was parallel to the whole trend of human thought since the Renaissance.   What has made all modern science and all modern philosophy is the appeal to fact, and, since all the facts that we know are in some sense facts of experience, that is the same as saying the appeal to experience.   The method of experiment, on which all our modern science depends, is simply the deliberate testing of experienced facts.   What was intellectually wrong with the Middle Ages was that men began with a dogmatic system that was taken for granted, on the authority of the past, and then proceeded to make deductions from it which became not only more and more complex, but also farther and farther removed from any verified and verifiable facts.   It is to be remembered that the dogmatic basis and the deductive method were almost as characteristic of medieval science and philosophy as of medieval religion.[1]

A new spirit of inquiry entered the world with the Renaissance. Many things contributed to it. The recovery of the language and literature of Greece by the Humanists was one factor, and the discovery of the new continent of America by Columbus was another, far apart as these things seem, for both went to show that the whole sum of knowledge was not contained in the traditional faith and the traditional philosophy. The human spirit began to inquire and explore in every direction, and it asked, not what had been believed and what had been said in the past, but what were the realities in every direction of human knowledge, the ascertainable facts ?

This is Bacon's principle throughout the *Novum Organon*, and he, more than any man, is the embodiment of the new spirit. All the way through he urges the appeal to fact, to experience, to experiment. ' *Experience* is by far the best demonstration, provided it adhere to the experiment actually made.'[2] ' Men have hitherto dwelt but little, or rather have only slightly touched upon, *experience*, whilst they have wasted much time on theories and the fictions of the imagination.'[3] ' Those who pursued only the probable reasons of things were carried about in a circle of arguments . . . and did not preserve the rigour of true inquirers, whilst none of them duly conversed with *experience* and the

---

[1] ' In the Middle Ages the method of authority, lording it over the human mind, dominated all sciences. A proposition of Aristotle, an utterance of Scripture, a dictum of the Fathers, a decision of a Council, settled officially, and for most men quite as fitly, a problem of physics, astronomy, or history as a problem of morals or philosophy.' – A. Sabatier, *The Religions of Authority and the Religion of the Spirit*, Introduction, xxii.

[2] *Novum Organon*, p. 406.

[3] Ibid., p. 438.

things themselves.'[1] 'The more ancient Greeks
. . . persisted in pressing their point and pursuing
their intercourse with nature ; thinking, as it seems,
that the better method was not to dispute upon the
very point of the possibility of anything being
known, but to put it to the test of *experience*.'[2] It is
true that Bacon did not invent the method of
induction, for men have argued inductively as well
as deductively since the beginnings of civilization,
but he did point out that far too much of the
reasoning of men in the past had been by deduction
from dogmatic assumptions, and that the time had
come when it ought to be much more by induction
from experimental facts.

The experimental method is, of course, simply an
appeal to experience. The scientist who makes an
experiment in the laboratory is trying to discover
the fact, the experienced fact ; not necessarily what
he expects to happen, or what he desires to happen,
or what he thinks ought to happen, but what does
actually happen, as far as we can know it and
experience it.

Now the appeal to experience, as against dogma,
began first of all, as we have seen, with physical
science, and it was natural that it should be so. It
is in the region of physical science that an experiment is most readily made. The facts of experience
can be most easily tested when they are the facts
that present themselves to the senses. Philosophy
went on with the dogmatic method ; it was only with
Descartes that the appeal to experience began, and
it was only with Kant, towards the end of the eighteenth century, that philosophy really awoke from
its dogmatic slumber. Theology went on with the
dogmatic method a little longer still, and it was only

---

[1] *Novum Organon*, p. 6.
[2] Ibid., p. 380.

with Schleiermacher, early in the nineteenth century, that theology definitely took its stand upon religious experience.[1]

Now it is surely a very striking fact, and yet it has scarcely ever been recognized at all in the past, that Methodism did, by a spiritual intuition, what Schleiermacher did consciously and constructively nearly a century later. Methodism instinctively grounded dogma upon religious experience. I do not suggest that Wesley and the early Methodists dreamed for a moment that they were engaged in a theological revolution. I do not think that they ever quite realized what they were doing, but they did it, for all that. They shifted the centre of authority from tradition to experience, and there is ample evidence of that in their writings.

It is not too much to claim that in the primacy accorded to religious experience Methodism carried forward the work of the Reformation to its legitimate and logical conclusion. Hugh Price Hughes, one of the dominant personalities among Methodists in the last generation, used to say that the final choice in religion was between Catholicism and Methodism. The saying expresses a considerable truth. The last issue is between the authority of tradition and the authority of experience, between a religion which stresses the continuity and validity of an ecclesiastical organization through which alone the individual soul can be certified of salvation by a priestly absolution, and a religion which stresses the continuity and validity of a spiritual fellowship, in which each individual soul is certified of salvation by the direct action of the Holy Spirit. In the one the whole emphasis is on the Church as an institution, and therefore upon its ministry and its rites, which are of primary importance, though

[1] A. Sabatier, *The Religions of Authority and the Religion of the Spirit*, p. 210.

some personal experience of religion is assumed or desired ; in the other the whole emphasis is upon the personal experience of religion, existing within that redeemed fellowship of men which is the Church, the ministry and the rites of which are, therefore, of secondary importance, though valued and almost vital assets to the life of the soul.

The absolute antithesis between Catholicism and Methodism is justified in the history of religious thought, for, as we have suggested, Methodism may be said to be the last stage of the Reformation, in which the primitive attitude of Christianity is finally recovered. It cannot be denied by those who accept Christianity at all, that the Christian religion began as a revelation of God in Christ, which became at once a spiritual experience in His first followers, who found God and redemption in Him, and a supernatural assurance of pardon and peace, through faith in Him, in their own souls. It was this actual experience which created both the New Testament and the Church, for the New Testament was the literature which recorded that experience, and the Church was the fellowship of men who possessed that experience. Then through long centuries the Christian religion was gradually paganized, and the banished conceptions of priest-hood and sacrifice reappeared – conceptions which belonged definitely to the primitive type of magical religion, persisting into paganism and Judaism. Early Christianity knew nothing of priesthood, except the completely spiritualized conception of Christ as the one great High Priest, and of all believers as a holy priesthood ; nothing of sacrifice, except the completely spiritualized conception of the Cross as the one great sacrifice for the sins of men, and of the devoted lives of believers as a living sacrifice from day to day. But now, from the third

KM

century onward, the ministry of the Church gradually became a priesthood, and the Eucharist a
sacrifice, in the pagan and primitive sense, and
religion came to rest upon the Church as an
organization which administered redemption, instead of upon the experience of the fellowship of
men who realized that redemption in their souls.
Thus all through the Middle Ages, and among
Catholics to-day, the final authority in religion is
the Church, backed by tradition, but not by the
earliest tradition of all.

The Reformation recovered the emphasis upon
experience, though the Reformers did not finally
base authority in religion upon it, but upon the
Bible. That was excusable enough at the time, and
perhaps inevitable. It was to the New Testament
that the Reformers went back, in their appeal
against superstition and in their recovery of primitive doctrine, and it was natural that they should
set up against the authority of the Church the
authority of the Scriptures. Some of the sectaries
and some of the mystics even then saw the better
way, and in the great Reformers, like Luther and
Calvin, the appeal to experience is always implicit.
But it is not surprising that theologians then sought
for a basis of authority as definite, as objective, and
as external as the Church, and found it in the Bible.

But the principle of the Reformation, carried out
to its logical issue, should go behind the Bible as
well as behind the Church ; it should go back to
the fact of revelation creating the fact of experience,
which is undeniably the primal, essential, creative
element in Christianity, if there is any truth in
Christianity at all. Now Schleiermacher, as I have
already suggested, worked this out as a theologian,
formally and constructively, but the early Methodists had done it a couple of generations before,

intuitively and instinctively, without realizing that they were doing so momentous a thing. But they did it, and perhaps the quatrain of Charles Wesley's which most completely embodies the spirit of Methodism is that in which he taught the Methodists to sing :

> What we have felt and seen
> With confidence we tell,
> And publish to the sons of men
> The signs infallible.

II

The next theological achievement of Methodism is that it made an end of Calvinism, for all practical purposes, and therefore laid a malign ghost that had haunted theology ever since the fourth century, for Calvinism is simply Augustinianism, revived and carried on to its remorseless issue by a man who was much more of a logician than St. Augustine, and much less of a mystic. The positive and praiseworthy element in Calvinism was the effort to attribute the *whole* of man's salvation to the grace of God. Then the question arose, Why are not all men saved ? The answer was, Because the grace of God is given to some, and not to all. Then, one step further back was taken, and the final position was reached. It is the will of God, the eternal decree of the Almighty, that grace should be given to some, who are the elect, and withheld from others, who are the reprobate.

Whitefield seems to have been greatly influenced by New England Calvinism when he was in America in 1740, where he became acquainted with Jonathan Edwards, and where, it must be remembered, there was a great revival of religion at the time among the Presbyterians and Independents, who were all Calvinists.   He wrote to Wesley, in the November of that year, lamenting the doctrinal differences which had already appeared between them. ' O that we were of one mind ! for I am yet persuaded you greatly err.' Wesley replied in a very conciliatory spirit, ' There are bigots both for predestination and against it.   God is sending a message to those on either side.   But neither will receive it, unless from one of his own opinion. Therefore, for a time, you are suffered to be of one opinion, and I of another '.

The division between the two friends was provoked by two publications of the Wesleys.   John Wesley had issued a sermon on ' Free Grace ' in 1739, and in 1740 there had appeared *Hymns and Sacred Poems* by John and Charles Wesley.   Now, Whitefield was offended by the doctrine taught in these publications.   In the sermon John Wesley wrote : ' Call it by whatever name you please, election, preterition, predestination, or reprobation, it comes in the end to the same thing.   The sense of all is plainly this – by virtue of an eternal, unchangeable, irresistible decree of God, one part of mankind are infallibly saved, and the rest infallibly damned ; it being impossible that any of the former should be damned, or that any of the latter should be saved.'   Then one of the hymns which appeared later in *Hymns and Sacred Poems* had been annexed to the sermon on ' Free Grace ', and some of the stanzas – the work of Charles Wesley – are a damning attack on the doctrine of predestination :

> *For every man He tasted death,*
> *He suffered once for all ;*
> He calls as many souls as breathe,
> And all *may* hear the call.

Thou canst not mock the sons of men ;
  Invite us to draw nigh,
Offer Thy grace to all, and then
  Thy grace to most deny !

Horror to think that God is hate !
  Fury in God can dwell !
God could a helpless world create,
  To thrust them into hell !

One result of the dispute was that some of the Methodists followed Whitefield, and there was a Calvinist party in the movement, which became influential amongst the evangelicals in the Church of England, amongst the Independents (many of the Societies established in association with the Countess of Huntingdon became, in effect, Independent Churches), and in Wales, under the leadership of Howell Harris. Whitefield and Wesley were personally reconciled, though each maintained his own doctrinal position, and when Whitefield died, in 1770, Wesley preached his funeral sermon.

About the time of Whitefield's death the Calvinist debate broke out with fresh fury, thanks largely to Rowland Hill and Augustus Montague Toplady, both very scurrilous controversialists. In the course of the dispute Toplady published *A Treatise upon Absolute Predestination, chiefly translated from the Latin of Zanchius.*[1] Wesley published an abstract of this in 1770, without note or comment, except one damning sentence at the end : ' The sum of all this is : One in twenty (suppose) of mankind are elected ; nineteen in twenty are reprobated. The

[1] Hieronymus Zanchi was an Italian born in 1516 at Alzano. He entered the order of Augustinian Canons at an early age, but the study of the writings of Luther, Melancthon, and Calvin led him to join the party of the Reformers, and he began to preach the Reformed doctrines in Lucca, but had to flee for his life. He lived at various periods of his life in Geneva, Strassburg, and Heidelberg, and once visited England. He was an ardent Predestinarian, and his contest with the Lutheran theologians of Marbach was one of the famous controversies of the age.

elect shall be saved, do what they will ; the reprobate shall be damned, do what they can. Reader,
believe this or be damned. Witness my hand,
A—— T——.' This reduced Toplady to hysterical
fury. He wrote of ' forgery ' that ought to commit
the criminal to transportation, if not to the gallows,
of Wesley's ' Satanic guilt ' and ' Satanic shame-
lessness ', and so forth. Wesley said of Toplady
and his associates, with absolute justice, that they
defended the doctrine of the decrees ' with arguments worthy of Bedlam and language worthy of
Billingsgate '. The temper shown by the advocates
of Predestinarian doctrine was, in fact, deplorable.
The warmth of feeling is curiously illustrated by the
fashion in which early Methodists were opposed
and persecuted. Most of the Dissenting ministers
seem to have disliked Methodism almost as much
as most of the clergy of the Established Church did.
But the opposition of the clergymen was generally
due to mere worldliness ; they did not like the
earnest preaching and the godly lives of Methodists,
which put them to shame. The opposition of the
Dissenting ministers, on the other hand, was due
in most cases to theological rancour ; they detested
the Arminian doctrine of the Methodists, and the
passionate proclamation of a universal gospel.
This might be endlessly illustrated from Wesley's
Journal and from the *Lives of the Early Methodist
Preachers*. The typical examples are those of clergymen, sometimes warm from the ale-house, who
primed the mob with drink to set upon the Methodists to the cry of ' Church and King ! ' and of
Dissenting ministers who were not nearly so brutal
in their methods of offence, but disputed bitterly
and angrily with the Methodists as to the doctrine
of election, and opposed their religious propaganda
on that score.

This temper of eighteenth-century Calvinism must be remembered if we are to understand the situation. The doctrine of reprobation was held in all its brutal and blasphemous crudity. Charles Wesley once quoted a terrible passage from Calvin's *Institutes* relating to the reprobate : ' God speaketh to them that they may be the deafer ; He gives light to them that they may be the blinder ; He offers instruction to them that they may be the more ignorant ; and uses the remedy that they may not be healed.'[1] And elsewhere the poet of Methodism records that during his exposition of a controverted passage of Scripture at Bristol one of his hearers ' even *called for damnation upon his own soul* if Christ died for all, and if God was willing THAT ALL MEN SHOULD BE SAVED '.

But sometimes the dispute about election took on an almost comic aspect. The following incident related in Wesley's *Journal* under the date May 20, 1742, illustrates both the rancour of the Calvinists and Wesley's own dry sense of humour. ' I over-took a serious man with whom I immediately fell into conversation. He presently gave me to know what his opinions were : therefore I said nothing to contradict them. But that did not content him : he was quite uneasy to know whether I held the doctrine of the decrees as he did ; but I told him, over and over, we had better keep to practical things, lest we should be angry at one another. And so we did for two miles, till he caught me una-wares, and dragged me into the dispute before I knew where I was. He then grew warmer and warmer, told me I was rotten at heart, and sup-posed I was one of John Wesley's followers. I told

[1] ' Ecce, vocem ad eos dirigit, sed ut magis obsurdescant ; lucem accendit, sed ut reddantur caeciores ; doctrinam profert, sed qua magis obstu-pescant ; remedium adhibet, sed ne sanentur.' – *Institutio*, lib. III, cap. 24, sec. 13.

him, "No, I am John Wesley himself!" upon which,

> Improvisum aspris veluti qui sentibus anguem
> Pressit,

he would gladly have run away outright, but, being the better mounted of the two, I kept close to his side, and endeavoured to show him his heart till we came into the street of Northampton.'

A paradoxical attempt has been made of late to minimize the opposition between Wesley and Calvin,[1] and to argue that the doctrine of Methodism is in essentials the doctrine of Calvinism. No doubt this odd line of argument has been influenced by Karl Barth's attempt to rehabilitate Calvinism. But surely there is here a real confusion of issues as well as a misuse of names. What are properly called the doctrines of grace are in no way the special property of Calvin. These truths were taught by Luther and all the Reformers, as they were taught long before by the Apostle Paul. That salvation depends wholly on the grace of God, that man is helpless without grace, and that faith is the acceptance of grace ; that of the whole of our redemption we must say with the Apostle, ' It is of faith, that it might be by grace ' – all this is no more Calvinism than it is Arminianism. It is evangelical Christianity, the religion of the New Testament, and the religion of the Reformers.

Arminianism has no quarrel with those essentially evangelical truths. When Toplady wrote the hymn ' Rock of Ages, cleft for me ', as a protest against Arminian doctrine :

> *Nothing* in my hand I bring
> Simply to Thy Cross I cling,

---

[1] Especially by Dr. George Croft Cell, in *The Rediscovery of John Wesley*, a book that is well worth reading on other grounds, for it is in many respects a very illuminating study.

the Methodists promptly adopted it, and ever since it has been used among them quite as frequently as among the communities that are historically Calvinist. Nothing in Arminian or Methodist doctrine has ever denied or doubted the absolute dependence of the soul upon the grace of God. As Arminius himself said, ' A rich man bestows on a poor and famishing beggar alms by which he may be able to maintain himself and his family. *Does it cease to be a pure gift because the beggar stretches out his hand to receive it ?* '

In the sermon on ' Free Grace ' Wesley teaches that the grace of God, which is the sole source of our salvation, is free in all and free to all. It does not depend on any power, or merit, or righteousness in man, on anything that he has done, or on anything that he is. These are not the cause of grace, but the effect of it. So far Wesley was at one with the Calvinists, and, indeed, it has been the insistence upon this positive part of the doctrine of grace that has always been the nobler strain in Calvinism. The deep sense of the sinfulness of sin, and the conception of grace as utterly undeserved, are the elements of Calvinism that have always been the source of its strength. The most convinced Arminian can rejoice in these truths. But there was another side to Calvinism, and it was this which Wesley fought with a passionate conviction. It meant a limited redemption : it denied the universal love of God, and the universal purpose of salvation. This, as Wesley urged with irresistible truth, is utterly dishonouring to God, if we believe that His name and His nature is love, and utterly destructive of the gospel of Christ, which proclaims a full and free salvation to all who will accept it.

To-day Calvinism is practically extinct. It only

survives among a few small sects like the Strict Baptists and the Plymouth Brethren, and in a few separatist Presbyterian Churches in the remoter parts of Scotland. It was Methodism that killed Calvinism, mainly by its impassioned evangelism, with its insistence that the grace of God was free for all who desired it. The diffusion of Charles Wesley's hymns through evangelical Christendom no doubt played a large part in the spread of Arminian doctrine.

This is illustrated, in an odd and significant way, by the fact that many verses of Charles Wesley's hymns are read and sung to-day without those who use them being at all aware of a polemic intention in the words. The battle with Calvinism has been won so completely that the original intention of many of the phrases in the hymns is quite un-realized, and the words are taken as the simple expression of what has become evangelical com-monplace. It seems natural to almost every religious mind in these days to declare that the redeeming love of God in Christ is for the whole world, and that the grace of God is offered to all men, whether they accept it in penitence and faith, or whether they reject it in their sin and selfishness and hardness of heart. But that was far from obvious to many who heard those hymns in the earliest days of Methodism. To many the pro-clamation of a universal gospel was a surprise, and to many it was an offence. Whenever the hymns speak of the universality of the gospel the words are a direct and deliberate attack on the militant Calvinism with which the early Methodists were faced. It is instructive to note the italicized words in the following hymn, as it was originally printed in the *Hymns on God's Everlasting Love*, in 1741 :

Father, Whose *everlasting love*
   Thy only Son for sinners gave,
Whose grace to *all* did *freely* move,
   And sent Him down *a world to save* ;

Help us Thy mercy to extol,
   Immense, unfathom'd, unconfined ;
To praise the Lamb who *died for all*,
   The *general Saviour of mankind.*

Thy *undistinguishing regard*
   Was cast on *Adam's* fallen race ;
For all Thou hast in Christ prepared
   Sufficient, sovereign, saving grace.

A world He suffered to redeem ;
   For all he hath the atonement made :
For those that *will not come* to Him
   The ransom of His life was paid.

Arise, O God, maintain Thy cause !
   The fulness of the *Gentiles* call ;
Lift up the standard of Thy cross
   And *all* shall own Thou diedst for all.

Apart from the italics, all those words and phrases would seem to nine hundred and ninety-nine Christians out of every thousand to-day the ordinary expression of a perfectly familiar and unchallenged truth. But every one of them denied what was passionately held by the eighteenth-century Calvinist – that Christ did *not* die for all men but only for the elect, and that it was *not* the will of God that all men should be saved, but only those whom He had destined to salvation by an eternal decree. It was the glory of Methodism to proclaim a universal gospel and a universal salvation, and here, as everywhere, the message is linked with penitence and faith and the glad certainty of a real experience of redemption, for the most moving protest against Predestinarian doctrine in Charles Wesley's hymns

is precisely in the lines which express the deepest
humility and at the same time the strongest assurance – the lines where he writes of the grace of God :

> Throughout the world its breadth is known,
>   Wide as infinity ;
> So wide it never passed by one,
>   Or it had passed by me.

III

The third contribution that Methodism has made
to theology consists in a new emphasis upon the
doctrine of sanctification and a new exposition of it.
Wesley himself regarded this as of the very first
importance. In a letter to Robert Carr Bracken-
bury, dated September 15, 1790, the year before
his death, Wesley says, ' This doctrine [of full
sanctification] is the grand *depositum* which God has
lodged with the people called Methodists ; and for
the sake of propagating this chiefly He appears to
have raised us up '.

There are three main sources in Wesley's writings
for his teaching on sanctification : first, his noble
little book, *A Plain Account of Christian Perfection*,
which ought to be recognized as a devotional
classic ; second, some of the sermons, especially
those on ' Christian Perfection', on ' Sin in Believers ' and on ' The Circumcision of the Heart ' –
the latter being especially interesting because it is
so early an expression of those views, for it was
preached at Oxford before the University in 1733 ;
and, third, numberless hymns, mostly by Charles
Wesley ; but it must be remembered that these
were sometimes criticized, sometimes revised, and
otherwise generally endorsed by John Wesley.

The first thing that will strike a careful student of

Wesley's doctrine is the essential sobriety of it. Here is no theological subtlety or devotional extravaganza. It is the plain teaching of Scripture, and the actual experience of believers, that is the standard throughout. Wesley would never have dealt with this matter of Christian Perfection at all if it had not been an actual element in the experience of believers, both as reflected in the New Testament and as discovered afresh in the lives of his own followers.

It must not be forgotten that there is an intensely practical side to this doctrine in another sense. There can be no real divorce between the life and the work, between the experience and the witness, either of the individual believer or of the whole fellowship of believers that we call the Church. The work and witness of the Church is always both energized and authorized by the hidden life of faithful souls. There is always a proportion between the holiness of the members of the Church and the success of the work of the Church. Whether in the primitive Church, or in early Methodism, or, indeed, in any period of spiritual revival, we must remember that it was the holiness of the lives of Christians that enforced and warranted the Christian appeal. The holiness of their lives – that is to say, their goodness, for holiness is nothing but supreme goodness. Holiness means loving God and loving men ; it means being pure, and pitiful, and kind, and generous, and unselfish. When we think of the passionate evangelism of the early Methodists we must remember that it would simply have gone for nothing if the holy lives of the early Methodists had not backed up the evangelistic appeal. When the world cannot deny that Christians live immeasurably better lives than the rest of men, then the world will listen to the Christian witness. The worldly man believes in deeds, and not in words, and he is quite right. He respects the realities of life and character and action. He will accept our proclamation of the gospel as a supernatural message only when it is warranted in his eyes by the supernatural goodness of the followers of Christ.

Wesley's doctrine amounts to this. Every part of life must necessarily be a sacrifice to God or to self. Our whole life, body and soul, every thought and every desire, as well as every act, ought to be yielded up to God. This spiritual surrender, as the habitual disposition of the soul, is what the Scriptures call holiness ; it is being perfect as our Father in heaven is perfect. It may, indeed, all be comprised in the one word love. It is to love God with all my heart and with all my soul and with all my mind and with all my strength, and my neighbour as myself. The negative side of it is a cessation from all sin. It does not mean perfection in the sense of freedom from ignorance, or from infirmity, or from temptation, but it does mean a full deliverance from sin, in the proper sense of the word ; that is, any voluntary transgression of the known will of God.[1] The experience is a spiritual state that is always capable of improvement ; one who is perfected in love may still grow in grace, and,

---

[1] I think Dr. Flew is right in his suggestion (in *The Idea of Perfection in Christian Theology*, p. 332) that some of the difficulties which beset Wesley's doctrine of perfection spring from ' an inadequate analysis of the nature of sin '. On the other hand, I think that Dr. F. R. Tennant is right in restricting the word ' sin ' to a voluntary transgression of a known law. Is it not really the difference between *sin* and *sinfulness* that is the issue ? There can be no doubt that Dr. Flew is on sure ground in stressing the fact that sinfulness in this sense, as rooted in self, is an endlessly subtle infection of the moral life. But Wesley did insist that those who were ' perfect ' ought to grow in grace, which means knowing more and more of our own unworthiness, and more and more of our need of the redeeming mercy of God. The hymns, in particular, constantly recognize the hidden root of sinfulness in self. ' O hide this *self* from me, that I No more, but Christ in me, may live ! ' ' Cleanse me from every sinful thought, From all the filth of *self* and pride ! '

indeed, grow more swiftly than he did before. There is no finality about it in the sense that it may not be improved. Nor is there any finality about it in another sense, for it may be lost, and it may be regained. It is always wrought in the soul by a simple act of faith, and consequently in a moment, though there is a gradual growth both preceding and following that instant.

Wesley thought that for the majority of believers the state of perfection was only reached in the hour of death. Yet he thought that there will be a progress in holiness on the other side of death. ' Can we reasonably doubt but that those who are now in Paradise, in Abraham's bosom – all these holy souls who have been discharged from the body, from the beginning of the world unto this day – will be continually ripening for heaven, will be perpetually holier and happier, till they are received into the kingdom prepared for them from the foundation of the world ? '[1]

As we have seen, Wesley did not deny that there might remain in those who were fully sanctified defects of knowledge and judgement and temperament, but he properly refused to call these sins. Nothing is sin, in the strict sense of the word, in which the will is not concerned. ' Christian perfection, therefore, does not imply (as some men seem to have imagined) an exemption either from ignorance, or mistake, or infirmities, or temptations. Indeed, it is only another name for holiness. They are two names for the same thing. Thus, every one that is holy is, in the Scripture sense, perfect. Yet we may lastly observe that neither in this respect is there any absolute perfection on earth. There is no perfection of degrees, as it is termed ; none which does not admit of a continual increase.

[1] Wesley's *Works*, VII, pp. 327–8.

So that how much soever any man has attained, or in how high a degree soever he is perfect, he hath still need to grow in grace, and daily to advance in the knowledge and love of God his Saviour.'[1]

In a letter dated May 12, 1763, Wesley wrote : ' Absolute or infallible perfection I never contended for. Sinless perfection I do not contend for, seeing it is not scriptural.' There is some ambiguity on this point. In *Brief Thoughts on Christian Perfection*, published in 1767, he says, ' I do not contend for the term sinless, though I do not object against it '. But there is no mistaking what Wesley really meant. He allowed that a perfectly sanctified believer could make mistakes, both in opinion and in practice, and that these were, in a sense, transgressions of the perfect law. But they were not voluntary transgressions, and they were not inconsistent with ' loving God with all the heart, so that every evil temper is destroyed ; and every thought and word and work springs from and is conducted to the end by the pure love of God and our neighbour '.[2]

It is unfortunate that holiness was thought of so largely, and especially by the opponents and critics of Wesley's doctrine, in terms of sinlessness, for the quality of holiness is not negative but positive. As Wesley said in a letter to Joseph Benson, ' Holiness is the love of God and man, or the mind which was in Christ '. He declared again and again that his doctrine of perfection simply meant loving God with all the heart, and your neighbour as yourself, and that this, like all else in the life of the soul, is wrought by the grace of God. It followed naturally in Wesley's judgement that when this was experienced it ought to be professed. The question naturally arises, Did he profess it himself ?

Apparently he did not, in so many words. There

[1] Wesley's *Works*, VI, pp. 5-6.   [2] *Minutes* of 1758.

is no definite statement of his that he had reached this great experience, and there are utterances, on the other hand, in which he expressly disclaimed it. In a letter dated March 5, 1767, answering an attack by the notorious Dr. William Dodd, in which there was the statement, ' A Methodist, according to Mr. Wesley, is one who is perfect, and sinneth not in thought, word, or deed ', Wesley wrote, ' Sir, have me excused. This is not " according to Mr. Wesley ". I have told all the world I am not perfect, and yet you allow me to be a Methodist. *I tell you flat I have not attained the character I draw*. Will you pin it upon me in spite of my teeth ? '

The nearest approach to an indirect profession of the experience on Wesley's part that I know of is in a footnote to one of his brother's hymns. Charles Wesley held strongly that the experience is only to be expected as the climax of long spiritual growth, and he held also that God sometimes arbitrarily withdraws or withholds His grace – a notion which was due to some of the mystics, and in which he was confirmed by the Prayer Book Version of Psalm xxvii. 16, 'O tarry thou the Lord's leisure '. In one of his hymns he wrote :

> Yet till Thy time is fully come
> I dare not hastily presume
> To snatch the perfect grace.

John Wesley appended to these lines the significant note : ' I dare say, " Now is the accepted time ".'

But, apart from what is implied in words like these, John Wesley never professed ' the perfect grace '. For my own part, I cannot doubt that he experienced it. Why did he not profess it ? Probably the reason is to be found in the peculiar publicity of his life. It must be remembered that the

LM

fierce light which beats upon a throne is nothing
to the minute and malignant scrutiny to which
John Wesley was subjected for fifty years together.
There must have been in his life from day to day
a thousand insignificant and innocent words and
actions which, distorted and exaggerated, might
have been alleged by his enemies against the high
profession of perfect love, had he made it. He knew
this, and was careful not to give the world any
unnecessary occasion to blaspheme. Doubtless in
his addresses to his Societies, in his heart-to-heart
conversations, in his more intimate letters, he would
speak more freely. In 1771 he wrote : ' Many
years since I saw that " without holiness no man
shall see the Lord ". I began by following after it,
and inciting all with whom I had any intercourse
to do the same. Ten years after God gave me a
clearer view than I had before of the way how to
obtain it, namely by faith in the Son of God. And
immediately I declared to all, " We are saved from
sin, we·are made holy by faith ". This I testified
in private, in public, in print : and God confirmed
it by a thousand witnesses.'

But, whether he himself professed it or not, Wesley
held generally that those who possessed the experience ought to bear witness of it at the right time
and in the right place. He wrote in 1787 to John
King, ' One great means of retaining the perfect
love of God is frankly to declare what God has given
you '.

There are very obvious dangers in any such profession. But it is only fair to point out that the
dangers are of exactly the same kind as in any sort
of religious testimony of a personal kind, and are
only to be avoided in the same way. There is a
danger in my professing that I know my sins forgiven, if there is any kind of self-confidence in the

assurance, but none if I feel all the time that the assurance is given by God to one who is unutterably undeserving of it. And so there is a peril in the profession of perfect love if it means that there is any self-satisfaction in the testimony, but none if the witness is borne with a perfectly humble heart and entirely to the glory of God.

There is a major difficulty which haunts Wesley's doctrine all the way through, due to the ambiguity of the words ' perfection ' and ' perfect ' – the use of which, by the way, he did not originate in this connexion. The doctrine is largely defined by reference to passages in the New Testament like Matthew v. 48, Philippians iii. 15, and 1 John iv. 17, 18, and there is an ambiguity in both the English and the Greek word, but more, perhaps, in the English ' perfect ' than in the Greek τέλειος. ' Perfect ' may mean either ' full-grown ' or ' flaw-less '. Perhaps one might say that the one sense is actual and historical, and the other ideal and absolute. The one means that the flower is perfect in the sense that the beauty of it is the full development of the plant ; the other means that the flower is perfect in the sense that it could not possibly be more beautiful than it is. The one sense is, therefore, dynamic, and the other static.

I would suggest that the main difficulty of Wesley's doctrine is that it moves so largely in the region of static conceptions. Wesley is not to be blamed for this, since it was due to the age in which he lived. But if there is one thing in which the world of thought has seen a real advance since the eighteenth century it is in that we have come to regard almost everything in the world in the aspect of a process rather than of a state. What does the whole change of thought represented by the conception of evolution really mean, on the largest scale ?   That instead of thinking of the universe as originating with all its different levels of existence separate and determinate from the beginning, so that soils, plants, animals, and men, for example, were at the very beginning what they are now, we rather think of the universe as one immense system of development, so that from its rudest beginnings to its last perfection, from the primitive nebula to the mind of man, it is all one vast process, in which the different *states* are really *stages* – the retrospective marking off of moments in a vital process rather than the original and unchangeable institution of different kinds of existence.   On one occasion at least Wesley himself realized this defect and difficulty in his teaching which has been mentioned. In the *Minutes* of 1770 he asks the question, ' Does not talking of a justified or a sanctified *state* tend to mislead men ?   Almost naturally leading them to trust in what was done in one moment ?   Whereas we are every hour and every minute pleasing or displeasing to God according to our works ; according to the whole of our inward tempers and our outward behaviour '.   In the doctrine of sanctification the modern mind would not stress so much a distinct passage from one sharply defined state to another, but rather the stages of a process of growth which is continuous, and expanding, and indeterminable.   Now that is surely in line with the facts of spiritual experience.   As a man is actually delivered from sin his soul becomes more sensitive to sin, and he realizes more and more of the subtle sinfulness of self, and so feels more and more his need of deliverance from sin.   As a man knows more of the grace of God he realizes more and more his need of further grace, and also more and more of the riches of the grace that he may claim in the name of Christ.   As a man grows in the knowledge

of God he realizes more and more that he may go
on growing immeasurably in that knowledge which
is life eternal.

And the very great value of Wesley's doctrine is
the way that he teaches that truth, in spite of what
I said about his being hampered by static conceptions. Here, it seems to me, his doctrine is strikingly
in line with the whole witness of Methodism.
Against the Calvinist doctrine of limited redemption the early Methodists passionately proclaimed
the limitless love and the limitless grace of God.
Exactly as they refused to admit any limit to the
possible range of redemption when thinking of the
race, so they refused to admit any limit to the actual
process of redemption when thinking of the individual. As it is God's will to save all men, and only
those are not saved who will not accept salvation,
so it is God's will to save those who are saved to the
uttermost, and the only reason why the work of
grace on us is imperfect is that we do not desire,
and will not submit, to be saved to the uttermost.
The grace of God can save me utterly, if I believe
that it can, and if I am willing to receive it, and that
salvation to the uttermost is a process that goes on
to infinity. It is a far cry from Wesley to St. Thomas
Aquinas, but there is a noble sentence in the *Summa
Theologica* : ' Since love is a participation in the
Holy Spirit, infused by God into the human soul,
no limit can be assigned to its increase in this
life.'[1]   The life of love is the life of holiness, and the
life of holiness is the life of the Holy Spirit within
us.   That is to say, the life of holiness is one with
the life and the love of God ; it *is* the life and love
of God in the soul of the believer.   But the life of

---

[1] ' Cum charitas sit Spiritus sancti participatio, a Deo in anima humana
facta, nullus eius augmento terminus praefigi in hac vita potest.' – *Summa
Theologica*, II, 2, qu. 24, art. 7.

God is an eternal life, and the love of God is an infinite love, and therefore a life and a love of which the believer may possess more and more through-out all time and all eternity. In God it is a life and a love which never began and never ends ; in us it is that same life and love which begins but never ends. As Charles Wesley wrote in those astonishing lines which might be said to condense the whole truth of this doctrine :

> We all shall commend
> The love of our Friend,
> For ever beginning what never shall end.

Wesley's teaching has at least rendered some great services to the whole concept of holiness. For one thing, it has refused assent to the medieval and Catholic conception of holiness as a thing almost apart from the ordinary life of men. I do not forget Brother Lawrence and some other saints, but it can scarcely be denied that the Catholic idea of holiness has been emasculated and exotic, ' a thing enskyed and sainted '. The highest life of holiness has been regarded as almost wholly withdrawn from the life of the world, a life of cloistered austerity and ecstatic contemplation. Wesley brought the whole ideal of holiness into the lives of ordinary men, where every homely duty is to become sacred, and every busy moment is to be dedicated to God.

Wesley's doctrine thus kept open a vista of sanctified experience for every believer. There was not a lower life with which most believers might be content, and a higher life to which a few saints might aspire. Every man who had repented and believed and yielded his life to Christ was to be one of those described in the quaint phrase that forms one of the headings in the *Collection of Hymns* of 1780, ' For Believers Groaning for Full Redemption '. He was to cry continually from the very depths of his heart :

> Thy nature be my law,
> Thy spotless sanctity,
> And sweetly every moment draw
> My happy soul to Thee.
>
> Soul of my soul remain !
> Who didst for all fulfil,
> In me, O Lord, fulfil again
> Thy heavenly Father's will !

But the most valuable element in Wesley's doctrine of entire sanctification, in my judgement, is that it refused to admit the defeat of the grace of God as a necessary or even as a normal event. It is strange that such a conception has been tolerated to the extent it has by most Christians in the past. The general thought has been that the soul might indeed grow in grace and goodness more and more, but that never in this life could we expect to escape wholly from the power of sin. Now, one has only to regard this from the higher side to see how intolerable a thought it is. Are we to believe that, while the grace of God can accomplish such miracles as utterly transform men's lives, it must nevertheless always fail before the end ? Why should it always fail in the last stage of all ? If the answer is, because of human infirmity, then that would as naturally and necessarily foil the grace of God at the beginning as at the end.

The real objection is that we shrink back from the thought of a perfect humanity, and it is precisely here that Wesley's necessary limitations, based upon the very nature of the experience, come into the

question.   It is not perfection in the absolute sense ;
there may be misjudgements in opinion and mistakes in practice.   But there may be, notwithstanding, perfect love toward God and toward man,
and that, as Wesley kept on saying all his life, is
what his doctrine meant.   I am bound in conscience, at this point, to bear witness that I have
known those among the people called Methodists
who, as far as human discernment could judge, had
attained this holy state.   When one has never been
able to detect, over a course of years, and while in
daily contact with a person, any word or act which
betrayed the presence of selfishness, or pride, or
anger, or any unworthy mood, it may surely be
concluded that for such a soul the prayer had been
answered :

O that with all Thy saints I might
  By sweet experience prove
What is the length, and breadth, and height,
  And depth of perfect love !

CHAPTER VI

THE LITERARY CONTRIBUTION

THE very significant contribution of Methodism to English literature has been generally ignored in the past. Doubtless this has been partly due, in the first place, to the fact that John Wesley and his brother Charles were not professed men of letters, and did not write ambitious works of a purely literary kind. It has been taken for granted, in consequence, that their literary achievement was negligible. This lack of recognition has been quite extraordinary. One or two casual illustrations of it may be given here. In the volume of the *Cambridge History of English Literature* entitled *The Age of Johnson*, which covers the period of the Wesleys, six pages of the fifteenth chapter are given to 'The Methodist Movement'. One page is devoted to Whitefield, who has positively no sort of literary significance at all; one to Fletcher, whose only claim to literary recognition must rest upon his forgotten controversial works; and one to James Hervey! Of Hervey it is enough to say that no sane person who is not a professed student of the by-ways of eighteenth-century religious literature will ever again read a page of his *Meditations among the Tombs*, or of anything else that he wrote. John Wesley is disposed of in a page and a half – about as much space as is devoted to George Smalridge. Charles Wesley is dealt with in twelve lines, and the *Lives of the Early Methodist Preachers* are not

mentioned at all. In Professor Saintsbury's contribution to the volume elsewhere a page is devoted
(and very properly devoted) to a critical estimate
of Blair's *Grave*. Charles Wesley was ten times more
of a poet than Blair, and his work is a hundred
times more significant in the history of our literature, and he is dismissed by Archdeacon Hutton in
four sentences. We are told by the same authority
that John Wesley was ' no poet '. In the highest
sense of the word he was not, of course ; but, then,
England only produced about three real poets
within his lifetime. He was at least as much a poet
as Collins, and a good deal more of one than Shen-
stone and Akenside, who all receive detailed and
serious treatment in the volume to which we are
referring. Another incidental illustration of the
extraordinary way that the Methodist contribution
to English letters has been ignored may be found
in the fact that in the *Handbook of English Literature*
by Austin Dobson there is no mention of either
John or Charles Wesley, except four lines in an
appendix. Now Austin Dobson knew the eighteenth century as well as any man of his generation,
and in the section dealing with the period between
1700 and 1785 he takes serious note of writers like
Atterbury and Warburton, Garth and Philips, but
entirely ignores the immensely more significant
work of the Wesleys in prose and verse.

Only one literary historian, so far as I know, has
ever perceived even the general debt of English
literature to Methodism, though it is there for all
to see. Writing of the religious side of Cowper's
genius, Dr. C. E. Vaughan has said that, while it
is memorable in itself, ' it is still more memorable
because it recalls the debt which English letters owe
to the religious revival, whether Evangelical or
Methodist, of the eighteenth century. As to the

ultimate effects of that revival on the general life of the country, there have been the inevitable differences of opinion.   But in literature, and especially in poetry, it would seem to have worked almost wholly for the good.   It disimprisoned a whole world of thought and feeling which had been fast chained beneath the hidebound formalism of the preceding era, and for want of which the land was perishing of inanition.   The poetic revival began to make itself felt within a few years after the Wesleys' life-long mission was inaugurated.   And, all things considered, it is difficult to resist the conclusion, not indeed that the religious movement was the cause of the literary movement, but that both sprang in the first instance from a common source ; and that, as years went on, the revival in literature was immeasurably quickened by finding an atmosphere charged with emotion and sympathy ready to receive it.   In Cowper's case, at any rate, the direct connexion of cause and effect can hardly be gainsaid.   And nothing could more clearly mark the gulf which separates him from Pope'.[1]   That is discerningly said, even if the express contribution of the Wesleys to our literature is not mentioned.

What are the plain facts ?   In the first place, the Wesleys produced the noblest body of devotional verse in the English language, which is in itself no trivial achievement, and their verse was entirely different, in style as well as in substance, from the poetry of the period.   Fifty years before the Lyrical Revival a new quality of simplicity and sincerity, of lyrical passion and imaginative daring, is found in these hymns.   Moreover, the prose of John Wesley and of some of the early Methodist preachers was equally independent of the stilted fashion of the period, and struck a new note in prose as

[1] *The Romantic Revolt*, p. 19.

definitely, if not as impressively, as the hymns did in verse. It would seem to be impossible that any one should deny or doubt this, if they know the writings of the early Methodists as well as the typical literature of the age, and yet it has hardly been recognized at all up to now.

This blindness on the part of men of letters is a singular fact, but it does not stand by itself. The literature of religion, and especially of religion in its evangelical aspect, is generally ignored by literary men until some great writer has been bold enough to set his seal of recognition upon it. It was remarked by Archbishop Trench that the greatest of all medieval hymns was never acknowledged as literature until Goethe used it with such dramatic effect in the cathedral scene in *Faust*, where the weeping Gretchen listens to the choir chanting :

> Dies irae, dies illa,
> Solvet saeclum in favilla.

There are many examples of this kind of belated recognition. John Bunyan was never conceded a place among the great writers of English prose until Macaulay wrote his famous essay on Southey's edition of *The Pilgrim's Progress*, with the characteristic paragraph at the end : ' Cowper said, forty or fifty years ago, that he dared not name John Bunyan in his verse, for fear of moving a sneer. To our refined forefathers, we suppose, Lord Roscommon's *Essay on Translated Verse*, and the Duke of Buckinghamshire's *Essay on Poetry*, appeared to be compositions infinitely superior to the allegory of the preaching tinker. We live in better times, and we are not afraid to say that, though there were many clever men in England during the latter half of the seventeenth century, there were only two minds which possessed the imaginative faculty in a very eminent degree. One of those minds produced the *Paradise Lost*, the other the *Pilgrim's Progress*.'

Evangelical religion has always fared badly in English literature, partly because it was so largely identified with Dissent, no doubt, but ultimately because the evangelical verities do not lend themselves to merely literary exploitation. Any gifted writer, even though he has no religion and no morals, can describe effectively the pomp and circumstance of Catholicism, for example, or any of the mere externalities of religion, but he cannot describe the passion of repentance and the simplicity of faith and the soul's devotion to Christ, unless he has known these in his own heart and life. Religious literature, even when it is the product of genius, and has the most unquestionable claim to rank as literature, necessarily stands rather apart.

There are other considerations of a less general kind. The very fact that the verse of the Wesleys was so unlike the typical poetry of the eighteenth century would alone have been sufficient to prevent any recognition of its value by the critics of the time. It was a formal and artificial period. Every writer desired above all things else to be ' correct '. What Théophile Gautier said of the literature of France applies to our own literature in the eighteenth century, when it was so strongly influenced by French writers like Boileau – it ' preserved a profound respect for rules, and never ran many literary hazards. . . . A writer trembled lest he should say something new, which could not be paralleled in authors of the best repute. . . . It would be wrong to attribute that imitative spirit to a lack of invention or of resources in the individual writer ; rather, it was a deference to the established mode, and a fear lest one should appear to be lacking in good taste '.[1] All that is emphatically true of English letters in the day of the Wesleys. Every writer of prose imitated Johnson ; every writer of verse imitated Pope. The general aim was to be polite, polished, and sensible. The age feared any passionate emotion – any ' enthusiasm ', to use the word in the contemporary sense – as it feared the small-pox. An odd illustration of this temper is found in the attitude of the eighteenth century to Shakespeare. It was overawed by him ; it could not and dare not deny his genius, but it felt obliged to apologize for him as ' wild ', and ' a child of Nature ', and so forth. It regarded him as a sort of noble savage who ran at large in the Elizabethan woods, and it thought in its heart that he would have been a much greater poet if he had had the advantage of living in a polite age, when his un-tamed genius could have acquired the exquisite polish which marked the verse of Mr. Pope. Now an age like that was not likely to appreciate the passionate and daring hymns of the Wesleys.

Since that time the literary recognition of the hymns has been prevented largely by a kind of snobbish pedantry that has often infected English letters. Methodism, like Dissent generally, was hardly respectable, and the literary pundits could not condescend to notice such a vulgar and fanatical movement, or its literature, if indeed it had any literature. Nearly all the literary critics and his-

[1] Cette nation si folle et si légère, au dire des observateurs, est celle qui a toujours conservé le plus profond respect pour les règles, et qui a le moins risqué en littérature. Dès qu'ils ont une plume à la main, ces Français si téméraires deviennent pleins d'hésitations et d'anxiétés ; ils tremblent de dire quelque chose de nouveau et qui ne se trouve pas dans les auteurs de bel air. Aussi qu'un écrivain ait la vogue, et tout de suite il paraît des nuées d'ouvrages taillés sur le patron du sien. On aurait tort d'attribuer cet esprit imitateur au manque d'invention ou de ressources individuelles ; ce n'est qu'une déférence à la mode, une crainte de paraître manquer de goût. – *Les Grotesques*, p. 58 (on Scarron).

torians have been under the influence of a vicious
tradition. It goes back to the Restoration prejudice
against the Puritans ; it was revived by the clerical
opponents of Methodism, who represented the early
Methodists as ignorant fanatics ; it persisted
through the eighteenth-century novelists and drama-
tists, who depicted every Methodist as a knave
or a fool, or an unsavoury combination of both.
Even Cowper, with all his evangelical sympathies,
dare not mention Whitefield plainly in his verse :

> Leuconomus (beneath well-sounding Greek
> I slur a name a poet must not speak).

Macaulay once complained that he had read his-
tories of the reign of George II in which there was
no mention whatever of the rise of Methodism, and
he expressed the pious hope that soon that breed of
writers would be extinct. The tradition lingered,
however, especially on the literary side, and Leslie
Stephen contrasted the Evangelical Revival un-
favourably with the Oxford Movement in this
respect, and said that Methodism had no literature
' possessing more than a purely historical interest '.
Now, restricting the consideration for the moment
to the poetical issue, it is difficult to imagine how
any man with any sense of literature at all could
think that the prim verse of Keble was to be named
beside the passionate raptures of Charles Wesley.
Yet Leslie Stephen was only repeating a general
belief, which is well enough illustrated by the fact
that, while there have been innumerable editions
of *The Christian Year* during the past hundred years,
the best of Charles Wesley's verse has never been
issued in a form to appeal to the reading public in
general : it has never appeared at all except in
hymnals for the use of Methodists.

The great revival in English literature is properly

dated from the publication of the *Lyrical Ballads* in
1798, though every one recognizes that in writers
like Gray, Burns, Blake, Thomson, and Cowper we
have the heralds of the new day.   What has never
been sufficiently admitted is that the Wesleys
sounded the new note forty years before Coleridge
and Wordsworth appeared.   I do not mean, of
course, that they brought in the new spirit of
romance that we associate with Coleridge and the
new feeling for Nature that we associate with
Wordsworth.   But I do mean that they recovered
a simplicity and sincerity of style, an imaginative
daring, and a spirit of passion and wonder, that
cannot be found in English letters for a couple of
generations before or after their day.   Many of
Charles Wesley's verses have a lyrical fervour and
a boldness of imagination that cannot be paralleled
anywhere in the eighteenth century.

The whole case for what has been said might rest
upon a single example, though there are many
others which might be given.   The magnificent
lines which are quoted below appeared in the
Hymns and Sacred Poems of 1749.   The hymn is an
exposition of Exodus xxxiii. 20, ' And the Lord
said, Thou canst not see My face ; for man shall
not see Me and live ', and the lines are influenced
throughout by some words of St. Augustine.   He
wrote in the *Confessions* (I. 5), ' Hide not Thy face
from me.   Let me die (that I die not) that I may
see Thy face ! ' and again in the *Soliloquies* (I),
' But why dost Thou hide Thy face ?   Haply Thou
wilt say, No man can see Me and live.   Ah, Lord,
let me die that I may see Thee ; let me see Thee
that I may die '.   (An earlier hymn, written in
1742, is entitled *Moriar ut te videam !*)   Apart from
some passages in Blake's poems (and Blake is an
anachronism and a portent), there is nothing in

English poetry with anything like the quality of these stanzas between Crashaw and Coleridge.

> I cannot see Thy face, and live,
> Then let me see Thy face, and die !
> Now, Lord, my gasping spirit receive,
> Give me on eagles' wings to fly,
> With eagles' eyes on Thee to gaze,
> And plunge into the glorious blaze !
>
> The fulness of my vast reward
> A blest eternity shall be ;
> But hast Thou not on earth prepared
> Some better thing than this for me ?
> What, but one drop ! one transient sight !
> I want a sun, a sea of light.

Let it be remembered that these lines were written in 1749 – that is to say, in the generation when Pope's *Essay on Man* and Johnson's *London* were the standards of poetic excellence – and then think of the poignant feeling, the imaginative boldness, the spiritual force, and, at the same time, the direct simplicity of Charles Wesley's stanzas.   If he had tried to write like every other poet of the period, how would he have expressed the exalted thought of those lines ?   Probably in some such fashion as this :

> Th' Eternal none may see and still survive,
> Howe'er devotion search and wisdom strive ;
> Then let the vision blest my spirit slay,
> And bear to better, brighter worlds away !
> Thus, borne on mighty pinions through the skies,
> Those azure fields to see with dazzled eyes,
> The soul, once past the realms of upper air,
> Immerse within the bright effulgence there.
>
> The rich reward that solid virtue yields
> Shall yet appear in th' Elysian fields ;
> But is there not, beneath these lower skies,
> Some greater recompense than meets our eyes ?

MM

> A scanty draught, a feeble gleam of light,
> Will not suffice us in our needy plight ;
> Th' ambitious mind demands a larger good,
> Full as the noonday's blaze, the ocean's flood.

Now these ridiculous lines are scarcely a caricature. Though I say it myself (as the proud author), they are a fair imitation of almost every poet in the middle of the eighteenth century, for they all wrote alike.

The poetical style of Charles Wesley is a remarkable phenomenon in our literature. It can hardly be disputed by any one who knows the writings in question, and possesses any critical discernment, that it is distinctly and strikingly the most modern style of the period. It is interesting to consider the reasons for this. One of the more technical reasons is that Prior was a favourite poet with both the Wesleys, and Prior's verse is much less stilted in its language, and much freer in its movement, than Pope's. In particular the trick of *enjambement* (which John Wesley learned from him) made Prior's verse more continuous and less epigrammatic than the characteristic poetry of the time. That is a detail, but it is not unimportant.

Much more important, of course, is the fact that both the brothers were steeped in knowledge of the Scriptures. I have given elsewhere many illustrations of their scholarly knowledge of the Greek Testament,[1] but here the point is that a thorough, reverent, and lifelong knowledge of the English of the Authorized Version made for a simple, natural, and forceful English style, both in prose and in verse. How thorough that knowledge of the Scriptures was may be illustrated by an example from Charles Wesley's verse. In one of his most famous hymns he wrote :

[1] In *The Hymns of Methodism in their Literary Relations* (Second Edition), pp. 16–38.

> Thou of life the fountain art,
>   Freely let me take of Thee,
> Spring Thou up within my heart,
>   Rise to all eternity.

The lines are simple and straightforward enough, and there is not the least effort to introduce any particular allusion, but there is a distinct reminiscence of Scripture in each line of the quatrain. The writer had in his mind the passage from Psalm xxxvi. 9, ' For with Thee is the fountain of life ', and this at once summons up the recollection of three other passages in Scripture in which there is the thought of a living spring – ' Let him take the water of life freely ' (Revelation xxii. 17) ; ' Then sang Israel this song, Spring up, O well ; sing ye unto it ' (Numbers xxi. 17) ; ' The water that I shall give him shall become in him a well of water springing up into eternal life ' (John iv. 14).

Many other examples might be quoted from Charles Wesley's verse of that intimate and instinctive familiarity with the Scriptures. Now it is not to be forgotten that this in itself is a literary equipment, for it means the knowledge of much more than a single book. No man who really knows his Bible is uneducated in the literary sense, for that knowledge means that he is familiar with an extensive, varied, and remarkable literature. As a matter of mere literary culture a man had much better have a really thorough and sympathetic knowledge of the Bible than a superficial acquaintance with the poetry and the fiction of the last thirty years, which is nearly all that some *littérateurs* of to-day seem to possess.

Moreover, the depth of religious feeling that characterizes much of the Bible makes inevitably for directness, simplicity, and passion, in literary expression. You do not look to the psalmists and the prophets, the evangelists and the apostles, for the literary artifice, the polite trifles in prose and verse, the stilted and self-conscious style, that marked so much of English literature in the days of the Wesleys. Instead, you find a religious experience and a spiritual passion that reaches its natural expression in words that are always simple, always direct, and that rise from time to time into a sheer ecstasy of feeling and of imagination.

Now all this applies in a double sense to the verse of Charles Wesley, for much of the quality of his hymns derives directly from a devout knowledge of Scripture, but most of it is due to the same kind of religious reality which is found in Scripture, but which had been rediscovered in the experience of the early Methodists. Here is the real secret. For the poetical style of Charles Wesley was not a deliberately designed mode ; it was the natural outcome of intense conviction and impassioned experience. It was this which released the emotional and imaginative impulses that the typical poet of the eighteenth century dare not admit into his verse, even if they chanced to visit his soul. The most casual glance at Charles Wesley's language would illustrate this . . . *triumph* . . . *passion* . . . *rapture* . . . *wonder* . . . *bliss !* Where, in any other eighteenth-century poet, do you find such words as these on every page ? If they are found at all, it is usually in some belittled and degenerate sense, but in Charles Wesley they maintain their exalted quality, for they are used of majestic themes and glorious experiences. The poetry of religion in his hands became again what all poetry in his generation had ceased to be, ' simple, sensuous, and passionate ', and the reason is that the literary quality and the spiritual quality of his verse are inseparably allied. Reality, simplicity, passion, the sense of wonder –

these things are present as literary attributes in the hymns, because first of all they are present as spiritual facts in the experience of the early Methodists. There is a phrase in Shakespeare – one of those amazing phrases that he throws out so casually – where he makes one of his characters say : ' They looked as they had heard of a world ransomed, or one destroyed : a notable passion of wonder appeared in them.' The early Methodists had that strange and apocalyptic outlook. They knew of a world destroyed by the sin of man, and ransomed by the death of Christ, and there was the source of the ' passion of wonder ' in these hymns. As Pascal said, there is always in the Gospel *quelque chose d'étonnant*, and the early Methodists realized in their own souls the astonishing quality of the evangelical message and the evangelical experience. Think of the constant echoes of it in these hymns . . . *unexampled grace !* . . . *unutterable praise !* . . . *rapturous awe !* . . . *amazing love !* . . .

The best of Charles Wesley's devotional verse was gathered together in the *Collection of Hymns for the Use of the People called Methodists*, which appeared in 1780. For more than a century it was the hymnal of Methodists (though supplements were added from time to time). It is almost impossible to exaggerate the importance of this fact. This book maintained the standard of Methodist experience and Methodist devotion for several generations ; it was to Methodists all that the Breviary is to Catholics, all that the Book of Common Prayer is to Anglicans. It expressed, and therefore both safeguarded and continually created afresh, the special type of Methodist piety. Some thirty years ago it was superseded by a new hymnal, and since the union of the various Methodist communities a few years ago there has been yet another hymnal, but still the psalmody of the Methodist people is drawn mainly from the hymns found in the 1780 volume.

The *Collection* of 1780 was an anthology, selected by John Wesley almost entirely from the great mass of his brother's verse. This gave it a quality which distinguishes it from almost every other hymnal in the world. It was a book with a literary character of its own. Charles Lamb has a famous phrase about books which are not books – *biblia a-biblia*. It is obvious that there are many printed volumes that are not books at all in any vital sense of the word. A dictionary or a directory is a book in the printer's and publisher's meaning of the term, but it is not a book in the higher sense, for as a mere compilation it does not possess a life and a unity of its own. There are some instances which are upon the border-line. Most of us would feel that works like Percy's *Reliques* and Palgrave's *Golden Treasury* deserve to be called books, for, though they are compilations, they do possess a kind of intellectual unity which gives them a soul. But most hymnals are mere collections made by an editor or by a committee, and they have no sort of unity or individuality that makes them worthy to be called books in the proper sense. The *Collection* of 1780, however, is a *book* – a literary entity. The fact that Charles Wesley wrote the greater part of the hymns, that John Wesley made the selection, and that practically all the hymns were thus the product of one religious movement, gave the book both a real unity and a character of its own which makes it unique. Every page of it breathes the essential spirit of Methodism – the experience, the passion, the wonder, and the joy which characterized the Evangelical Revival.

Lest the high estimate of the hymns of Methodism

which has been expressed in these pages should be
regarded as mere prejudice on the part of a fanatical
Methodist, let me quote a couple of judgements
that have been passed upon the *Collection* of 1780 by
two distinguished men, one a Unitarian and one a
Congregationalist. Dr. Martineau once remarked,
in a letter to Miss Winkworth, that this volume was,
' after the Scriptures, the grandest instrument of
popular religious culture that Christendom has ever
produced '. And Mr. Bernard Manning has
recently said that it ' ranks in Christian literature
with the Psalms, the Book of Common Prayer, the
Canon of the Mass. In its own way it is perfect,
unapproachable, elemental in its perfection. You
cannot alter it except to mar it ; it is a work of
supreme devotional art by a religious genius '.[1]

Apart from the purely literary issue, it ought to
be remembered that the hymns of the Wesleys were
a portent in the religious life of the country. There
are many contemporary references to the singing
of hymns by the early Methodists as a striking
novelty, for psalmody had held only a small place
in worship in the early years of the eighteenth
century, and, moreover, such hymns as existed in
English were generally of the poorest quality. The
hymns of Methodism lifted the whole of English
psalmody on to a new level. John Wesley said in a
letter to a friend, dated September 20, 1757,
describing the worship of the Methodists, that ' the
solemn praises of God ' among them were ' not
interrupted either by the formal drawl of a parish

---

[1] I cannot deny myself the pleasure of saying here how much gratitude
and how much admiration I feel for Mr. Bernard Manning's writings – all
too scanty, alas ! – especially his booklets *Christian Experience throughout the
Centuries* and *Some Hymns and Hymnbooks*, and the article I have quoted, which
appeared in the *London Quarterly and Holborn Review* in 1933. Mr. Manning
is a distinguished scholar and a delightful writer, but he is more, for he
himself possesses a real tincture of the religious genius which he attributed
to Wesley.

clerk, the screaming of boys who bawl out what they neither understand nor feel, or the unreasonable and unmeaning impertinence of a voluntary on the organ. When it is seasonable to sing praise to God they do it with the spirit and the understanding also, not in the miserable, scandalous doggerel of Sternhold and Hopkins, but in psalms and hymns which are both sense and poetry, such as would sooner provoke a critic to turn Christian than a Christian to turn critic'. It is not always remembered that the only psalmody in English congregations until the rise of Methodism did consist of those very pedestrian renderings of the Psalms to which Wesley referred. It is true that Dr. Watts had begun to show a better way, and his name will always hold a high place in English hymnology, both as a pioneer and also on account of the abiding value of a dozen fine hymns that he wrote, among many other verses that are little more than doggerel. But there can surely be no kind of parallel between Dr. Watts and Charles Wesley, except for the one hymn, 'When I survey the wondrous cross'. Otherwise no comparison is possible between the hymns by the two writers, as to religious or literary quality ; neither is there any parity whatever as to the extent of their influence upon the religious life of English Christendom.

John Wesley had a just sense of his brother's poetical gift. There is a passage in his *Journal*, under the date December 28, 1789, in which he records that he read the *Life of Mrs. Bellamy* – ' a very pretty trifle '. ' Abundance of anecdotes she inserts, which may be true or false. One of them concerning Mr. Garrick is curious. She says : " When he was taking ship for England, a lady presented him with a parcel, which she desired him not to open till he was at sea. When he did he found Wesley's hymns, which he immediately threw overboard." I cannot believe it. I think Mr. Garrick had more sense. He knew my brother well ; and he knew him to be not only far superior in learning, but in poetry, to Mr. Thomson and all his theatrical writers put together. None of them can equal him, either in strong nervous sense, or purity and elegance of language.'

Many of the hymns of the Wesleys are now in familiar use throughout the whole of the English-speaking world. Such are : ' O for a thousand tongues to sing ! ' ; ' Jesus, the name high over all ' ; ' Jesu, Lover of my Soul ' ; ' Would Jesus have the sinner die ? ' ; ' O Love Divine, what hast Thou done ? ' ; ' Come, Thou long-expected Jesus ' ; ' Jesus, the Conqueror, reigns ' ; ' Earth, rejoice, our Lord is King ' ; ' Lo ! He comes with clouds descending ' ; ' O Thou who camest from above ' ; ' Love Divine, all loves excelling ' ; ' Thou hidden love of God, whose height ' ; ' Thee will I love, my Strength, my Tower ' ; ' Soldiers of Christ, arise ! ' ; ' O for a heart to praise my God ! ' ; ' Lo, God is here, let us adore ! ' ; and many others.

The writings in verse of John and Charles Wesley occupy thirteen volumes. Nearly the whole of this mass of work consists of hymns, and nineteen-twentieths of it, or more, is the work of the younger brother. Now it is a natural impossibility for the whole of such an enormous quantity of verse to be on a high level of inspiration, or anything like it. The greater part of it is mere versification of the commonplaces of evangelical religion, but most of it is interesting, a good deal of it is scholarly, and a hundred or more of the hymns may fairly be said to reach a very high level as devotional poetry. The very best of Charles Wesley's hymns are worthy to stand beside the greatest of the Latin hymns of the Middle Ages, and the greatest of the German hymns of the Reformation and of Pietism.

While there has been such a grudging recognition, generally, of the literary quality of the hymns of early Methodism, it is significant that a great many of them have been appropriated and used by all the Churches. That is especially true of the hymns for the great festivals of the Christian year. John Wesley said in a letter to Thomas Wride on January 22, 1774 : ' Some of my brother's Christmas hymns are some of the finest compositions in the English tongue.' That judgement might be extended to many of Charles Wesley's hymns for the festivals of Christendom. Wherever the English language is spoken, these hymns are heard in the course of the ecclesiastical year – ' Hark ! the herald angels sing ', at Christmas (Charles Wesley wrote ' Hark ! how all the welkin rings, Glory to the King of Kings ! ' and it is a pity that the original cannot be restored, for it is better poetry and more true to Scripture) ; ' Christ the Lord is risen to-day ', at Easter ; ' Hail the day that sees Him rise ', at Ascensiontide ; and ' Granted is the Saviour's prayer ', at Whitsuntide. It is rather a striking fact that it was not the Oxford Movement but the Evangelical Revival that gave these great hymns of praise for the festivals of the Church to the English language.

There are some other hymns for special seasons of the Church and of the year which are not as well known outside Methodism, perhaps, as these last, but which are of an equally noble character, like ' Come, Thou long-expected Jesus ', ' Stupendous height of heavenly love ', and ' Glory be to God on high ', for the season of Advent ; ' Our Lord is risen from the dead ! ' at Easter ; and ' God is gone

on high ', on Ascension Day.   There are no hymns
in English that can be compared for a moment
with Charles Wesley's hymns for Trinity Sunday,
such as ' Hail ! holy, holy, holy Lord ! ' and
' Father, in whom we live '. So, again, there are
no Eucharistic hymns in the language which surpass
' Victim Divine, Thy grace we claim ', ' Lamb of
God, whose dying love ', and ' Come, Thou everlasting Spirit '.   The Watchnight Service held on
the last night of the year (which has been widely
adopted by other Churches) has familiarized many
English people with a hymn that stands alone in its
appropriateness for that particular hour – ' Come,
let us anew Our journey pursue '.   There are no
finer morning and evening hymns than ' Christ,
whose glory fills the skies ' and ' All praise to Him
who dwells in bliss ', and I should like to associate
with them the two beautiful hymns entitled ' Before
Work ' and ' To be Sung at Work ', ' Forth in Thy
Name, O Lord, I go ', and ' Servant of all, to toil
for man '.   The funeral hymns are not now much
used or much known, because other-worldliness is
unfashionable in our days, but the note of spiritual
triumph over the last enemy has never been
sounded more finely than in hymns like ' Come, let
us join our friends above ' ; ' What are these
arrayed in white ? ' ; ' Rejoice for a brother
deceased ! ' ; ' Hark ! a voice divides the sky ' ;
and ' Happy soul ! thy days are ended '.   Finally,
in dealing with these hymns on special themes and
for special occasions, let me say that (though it is
not widely known) ' Eternal Lord of earth and
skies ' is the greatest missionary hymn in the
language.

Charles Wesley wrote hymns dealing with almost
every aspect of the Christian faith and almost every
experience of the Christian life.   Every event in his

own life and in the lives of his friends was celebrated by the composition of a hymn. He set himself also to write hymns for all sorts of people under all sorts of conditions. A quaint list of titles might be compiled to illustrate all this. Here are some : ' For a Sick Child ', ' On Sending a Child to the Boarding-School ', ' For a Persecuting Husband ', ' For an Unconverted Wife ', ' A Wedding Song ', ' On Going to a New Habitation ', ' On a Journey ', ' For a Family in Want '. Some of the titles recall the dangers that beset the early Methodists in their work for God, such as, ' To be sung in a Tumult ', ' Written after a Deliverance from a Tumult ', ' Written on a Journey in Peril of Robbers ', ' Written on going to Wakefield to answer a Charge of Treason ', and ' Occasioned by an Irish Judge sentencing me in my absence to Transportation ' ; and some recall the amazing evangelism of those days, such as, ' The Collier's Hymn ', ' For the Kingswood Colliers ', ' After Preaching to the Newcastle Colliers ', and (most pathetic of all) ' For Condemned Malefactors '. Many a penitent went to the gallows at Tyburn with the words of one of these last hymns on his lips :

> O might we with our closing eyes,
> Thee in Thy bloody vesture see,
> And cast us on Thy sacrifice !
> Jesus, my Lord, remember me !

Some of the finest of the hymns are translations from the German by John Wesley. He had not the lyrical gift of his brother, and, though he wrote a few original hymns, perhaps none of these is of the first rank, except ' Peace, doubting heart ! my God's I am '.[1] But he was an incomparable trans-

[1] There are conclusive reasons, I think, for believing that this hymn is one of John Wesley's compositions, if the critical principles are applied which I have outlined in *The Hymns of Methodism in their Literary Relations* (Second Edition), pp. 129–35.

lator. Emerson said that the finest hymn in the English language was ' Thou hidden love of God, whose height, Whose depth unfathomed, no man knows ', which is Wesley's version of Tersteegen's ' Verborgne Gottes Liebe du '. Several other of Wesley's renderings are really supreme examples of skill in translation. Let any one compare the original of Rothe's ' Ich habe nun den Grund gefunden ' with Wesley's version of it, ' Now I have found the ground wherein, Sure my soul's anchor may remain '. The rendering is amazingly literal, almost as literal as a prose translation could be, and yet the hymn is as much of a religious poem in English as it is in German, if not more so.

It should be noted that in all this John Wesley was a pioneer. In the middle of the eighteenth century every educated Englishman knew French, but German was almost as unknown as Russian. It was only at the very end of the century, when the fame of Goethe and Schiller among the poets, and Kant and Fichte among the philosophers, was beginning to reach the English intelligentsia, that Englishmen began to learn German. Practically the first translations of German poetry were by Coleridge, Scott, and Shelley. Wesley was fifty years ahead of his contemporaries in his knowledge of German, though here, as everywhere else, the motive was not literary but religious. He learned German in order to converse with the Moravians on board the ship that carried him to Georgia. But his knowledge of the language was used to introduce English Christians to the treasures of German psalmody, in the devotional poetry of Scheffler, Gerhardt, and Tersteegen, as well of Moravians like Rothe and Zinzendorf.

The prose writings of John Wesley and of the early Methodist preachers, remarkable as they are, have been almost as unnoticed by literary historians and literary critics as the verse of Charles Wesley, at least until quite recent times. Wesley's *Journal* is surely as important as Pepys's *Diary* – as interesting in itself, and as necessary to the understanding of the period – and yet no one outside of the circle of Wesley's own followers ever appreciated it until Edward FitzGerald came across it, and wrote to Professor Cowell, ' Another book I have had is Wesley's *Journal*. If you don't know it, *do* know it : it is curious to think of this Diary of his running almost coevally with Walpole's Letter-Diary, the two men born and dying too within a few years of one another, and with such different lives to record. And it is remarkable to read pure, unaffected, and undying English, while Addison and Johnson are tainted with a style which all the world imitated '. In spite of this discerning utterance there was no popular edition of Wesley's *Journal*, and no real interest in it on the part of the general reader, until, years later, Mr. Augustine Birrell wrote a well-known essay, in which (though he said that ' as a writer Wesley has not achieved distinction ') he spoke enthusiastically of the interest and vitality of the *Journal*, and described it as ' the most amazing record of human exertion ever penned or endured '.

As to the distinction of Wesley's writing, however, FitzGerald was much nearer the truth. For the significance of the prose of the early Methodists is only less remarkable than that of their verse. In the case of John Wesley this is rather masked by his use of a few archaic forms, like ' hath ' for ' has ' and ' wrote ' for ' written ', which give an old-fashioned air to some of his sentences. In spite of that detail, the contrast between his style and the typical prose of the eighteenth century is there for all who have eyes to see it. It must be remembered

that English prose in Wesley's day was dominated
first by Addison, and a little later by Johnson,
almost as absolutely as English verse was dominated
by Pope.   Consider, for the sake of the contrast with
Wesley and the early Methodist preachers, the style
of these two writers who were so admired at the
time as masters of English prose.

There is a penetrating criticism of Addison in
one of De Quincey's writings. ' Addison, in particular, shrank from every bold and every profound
expression as from an offence against good taste.
He dared not for his life have used the word
" passion " except in the vulgar sense of an angry
paroxysm.   He durst as soon have danced a horn-
pipe on the top of the Monument as have talked of
" rapturous emotion ".   What *would* he have said ?
Why, " sentiments that were of a nature to prove
agreeable after an unusual rate ".'   In one of his
essays Hazlitt has criticized Addison with almost
equal insight.   He complains that Addison's style
was ' not indented, nor did it project from the
surface.   There was no stress laid on one word
more than another – it did not hurry on or stop
short, or sink or swell with the occasion ; it was
throughout equally insipid, flowing, and harmon-
ious, and had the effect of a studied recitation rather
than of a natural discourse '.

There is another passage in one of Hazlitt's writings where he points out with equal discernment
the faults of Johnson's style. ' What most distinguishes Dr. Johnson from other writers is the pomp
and uniformity of his style.   All his periods are cast
in the same mould, are of the same size and shape,
and consequently have little fitness to the variety
of things he professes to treat of.   His subjects are
familiar, but the author is always upon stilts. . . .
The fault of Dr. Johnson's style is, that it reduces

all things to the same artificial and unmeaning level. It destroys all shades of difference, the association between words and things.' Macaulay, in a famous essay, has similarly described Johnson's ' constant practice of padding out a sentence with useless epithets, till it became as stiff as the bust of an exquisite, his antithetical forms of expression, constantly employed even where there is no opposition in the ideas expressed, his big words wasted on little things, his harsh inversions, so widely different from those graceful and easy inversions which give variety, spirit, and sweetness to the expression of our great old writers '.

These criticisms are undeniably just, and hardly any one to-day would challenge them. But let it be remembered for the moment that Addison and Johnson were vastly admired and sedulously imitated by every one who aspired to write well in the middle of the eighteenth century. Now contrast their style with John Wesley's. Let us take a passage from his writings, not on a religious issue, since this would necessarily introduce a phraseology which could not be easily paralleled in the other writers, but one that is simply concerned with a question of humanity, and then translate it into the dialect of Addison and Johnson.

Wesley wrote, in his *Thoughts upon Slavery* : ' The grand plea is, " They are authorized by law ". But can law, human law, change the nature of things ? Can it turn darkness into light, or evil into good ? By no means. Notwithstanding ten thousand laws, right is right, and wrong is wrong still. There must still remain an essential difference between justice and injustice, cruelty and mercy. So that I still ask, Who can reconcile this treatment of the negroes, first and last, with either mercy or justice ?

' Where is the justice of inflicting the severest evils on those that have done us no wrong ? of depriving those that never injured us in word or deed, of every comfort of life ? of tearing them from their native country, and depriving them of liberty itself, to which an Angolan has the same natural right as an Englishman, and on which he sets as high a value ? Yea, where is the justice of taking away the lives of innocent, inoffensive men ; murdering thousands of them in their own land, by the hands of their own countrymen ; many thousands, year after year, on shipboard, and then casting them like dung into the sea ; and tens of thousands in that cruel slavery to which they are so unjustly reduced ? '[1]

If John Wesley had tried to write like Addison, he would have expressed this in some such fashion as the following : ' A great plea is made, that the law allows of it. But it is not rational to think the law of man can change the nature of things. None believe that the laws can turn night into day, or vice into virtue. All know that a course of action is judged just or unjust in spite of all laws that were ever made by man. Sure there is a vast difference between justice and injustice, and no less betwixt cruelty and acts of mercy. And who can make the usage of negroes seem to accord either with mercy or with justice ?

' How is it right to put the worst of evils upon those who did no wrong to us ? and deprive them (though never in any way injurious to us) of every comfort of their life ? They are brought from their native land, and their liberty taken away, which is as proper to a native of Angola as to one of England, and doubtless as prized by him. There is little of justice in taking the lives of these innocent

[1] Wesley's *Works*, XI, p. 70.

people ; for thousands perish in their own land by the hands of their own countrymen ; many more on shipboard (those that die being cast into the sea) ; and vast multitudes at last in the horrid slavery we have reduced them to.'

If John Wesley had tried to write like Johnson he would have written the passage something like this : ' The principal argument here advanced is, that such practices have the solemn authorization of law. It is proper to inquire whether the essential nature of things may be altered by the laws of man ? There is no authentic power in human law to change darkness into light, or to convert evil into good. Justice retains its character of equity, and injustice its perverted nature, despite the existence of every legislative enactment. There must remain, through all the course of time, and through all the change of events, a fundamental difference between the standards of justice and those of injustice, and an immense distance between the impulses of cruelty and the sentiments of compassion. I know not how this treatment of the negroes can be thought to accord either with the counsels of mercy or with the dictates of justice.

' Justice is not exhibited by inflicting the severest evils upon those who have not wronged us, and by depriving men who never injured their oppressors, in word or in act, of all the consolations of human life ; in exiling them from their native land, and depriving them of that liberty to which, like an Englishman, an Angolan has a natural right, and on which he sets as exalted a value. Justice is not demonstrated in taking the lives of men who are innocent and inoffensive, by the slaughter of thousands of them in their own land, through the barbarous complicity of their own countrymen, by the loss of thousands more in the hardships of the

voyage and the perils of the ocean, and finally by
the death of myriads in the endurance of the horrors
of that slavery to which they are reduced without
justice and condemned without hope.'

In comparison with Wesley's simple, vigorous,
and idiomatic English the prose of Addison would
strike any one to-day as slightly archaic, rather
toneless, and, in Hazlitt's phrase, 'insipid', and that
of Johnson would seem ponderous and pompous
throughout. But these were the models in the
middle of the eighteenth century. Johnson himself said, 'Whoever wishes to attain an English
style, familiar but not coarse, and elegant but not
ostentatious, must give his days and nights to the
volumes of Addison', but most writers of Johnson's
period did not take his advice. It would have been
better if they had, for they tried rather to imitate
the style of 'the great lexicographer' (as Miss
Pinkerton did half a century later), with very
unhappy results.

Wesley expressed his own convictions on the
matter of style more than once, and in the fashion
that we should expect. He said in a letter to Samuel
Furley on October 11, 1764, 'I have no prejudice
for or against any writer ; but I may say, without
much vanity, I know a good style from a bad one,
and it would be a shame if I did not, after having
spent five-and-forty years (with some natural understanding, much attention, and a free acquaintance
with many eminent men) in reading the most
celebrated writers in the English tongue'. He
spoke of his own prose style in the Preface to the
Sermons on Several Occasions, published in 1788. He
says that he writes as he does from deliberate choice.
' I could even now write as floridly and rhetorically
as even the admired Dr. B——' (this is evidently
the Scottish preacher Dr. Blair, whose sermons

were immensely admired at that date, and are now totally forgotten), ' but I dare not . . . I dare no more write in a fine style than wear a fine coat.' He goes on to say that if the language of a preacher is ' plain, proper, and clear, it is enough ' ; that he should imitate both the matter and the manner of the oracles of God, and ' if he would imitate any part of these above the rest, let it be the First Epistle of St. John '.

Wesley did a great deal for popular culture by way of the fact that he created a new class of readers in the Methodist people, and provided them with literature, in his own and his brother's writings, in the *Arminian Magazine*, in the *Christian Library*, and in numerous other reprints and abridgements of books, devotional and otherwise. Over four hundred of these have been catalogued. It is known that Wesley made some £30,000 by his publications, and he devoted all of it to religious and charitable uses.

It was through the medium of the *Arminian Magazine* that we come to possess what is, next to Wesley's own writings, the most remarkable example of English prose produced by early Methodism, in the *Lives of the Early Methodist Preachers*. Wesley asked many of his older preachers to write an account of their life and experience, and most of these autobiographies appeared in the *Arminian Magazine* between 1778 (the year of its commencement) and 1811. They were collected by Thomas Jackson and published in three volumes in 1837–8. Five editions of one kind or another have appeared since.

It is difficult to write honestly of this extraordinary collection of memoirs without seeming extravagant. Wesley's purpose in getting them written was a purely religious one ; he wanted an account of the

religious experience of these men. From that point
of view they are eminently worth study, as devotional literature, and also as a source for the student
of the psychology of religion.[1] But there is a great
deal of interest in these lives apart from the purely
religious issue. There is nothing more romantic,
in fact, in the literature of the eighteenth century
than such memoirs as those of Sampson Staniforth,
Silas Told, and John Nelson. Staniforth was a
drunken young reprobate who enlisted in the army,
and fought in Flanders. He narrowly missed death
at the hands of the provost-marshal on more than
one occasion, to say nothing of the perils of the
battlefield. He was wonderfully converted, returned to England, and became one of the early
Methodist preachers. Silas Told was a sailor for
some years, mostly on slave-ships ; he had strange
experiences of mutiny, piracy, and shipwreck ; how
R. L. Stevenson would have delighted in Told's
autobiography if he had only known it ! Told was
awakened to a knowledge of the things of God
under a sermon by Wesley, but he continued in
great distress of spirit for some years before he was
able to find peace. After he had lived for some
time in London he heard Wesley preach at the
Foundery one morning at five o'clock on the text,
' I was sick and in prison, and ye visited me not '.
The words went home to his heart, and he devoted
the rest of his life to the wretches in the London
jails. He tells some amazing and pathetic stories
of his experiences in those fearful places. John
Nelson was a Yorkshire stonemason. He heard
Wesley preach one day on Kennington Common,
and gave his life to God. He became one of the

[1] They are used to good purpose in Professor Dimond's book on *The
Psychology of the Methodist Revival*, and in Dr. A. Caldecott's brochure, *The
Religious Sentiment, illustrated from the Lives of Wesley's Helpers*.

best of Wesley's preachers. There is not so much of the extraordinary in his record as in those of Staniforth and Told ; the most exciting things that happened to him were experiences of mob violence and clerical persecution in his career as a preacher. But it is a most interesting life.

All these early preachers have the same gift as Wesley had (some of them have it in an even greater degree) for writing pure, idiomatic, un-affected English, which stands in the most complete contrast to the pompous prose that was the literary fashion in their day – a fact which is surely very suggestive. My contention in these pages is, in short, that though the contribution of Methodism to English literature has never been adequately acknowledged in the past, it was quite a consider-able one. The hymns of Methodism are the finest body of religious verse in the language, and they constitute one of the three great schools of hymnody that the world possesses, standing worthily beside the great Latin hymns of the Middle Ages, and the great German hymns of the sixteenth and seven-teenth centuries. For while a solitary author has occasionally written a great hymn from time to time, there have unquestionably been only three great periods of sacred song in the West, and they derive from medieval Catholicism, from the period of the Reformation in Germany (extended suffi-ciently to include Pietism), and from Methodism. Moreover, the hymns of the Wesleys sounded the lyrical note of simplicity and wonder and passion that had been lost since the days of Crashaw and Vaughan, and that was only recovered with the advent of Coleridge and Wordsworth. Still further, the prose of John Wesley and some of the early Methodist preachers showed as significant a recovery of simplicity and sincerity as did the verse of

Charles Wesley. Both in prose and in verse, there-fore, and both as regards substance and style, the writings of early Methodism are really a very significant episode in our literature, and, indeed, something of a portent.

It may be said that all this is merely the expression of personal preferences, and we may be reminded that there is no arguing about tastes. But it must be remembered that there are such things as literary standards, after all. No unprejudiced jury of literary men who had read the works in question would deny that Wesley's *Journal* is one of the most important and one of the most interesting books of the century, and that his prose style is as powerful and precise an instrument as Swift's ; that Charles Wesley is the greatest of all English writers of devotional verse, and that his hymns are really a landmark in the renaissance of English poetry. No candid and competent critic, when once his attention had been called to the writings in question, could possibly challenge these judgements.

CHAPTER VII

THE SOCIAL CONTRIBUTION

IT is rather significant that the considerable contribution of Methodism to social progress has been generally admitted. That kind of achievement is visible and tangible, and every one to-day believes in it, however uncertain he may be about spiritual processes and spiritual results. John Richard Green, in a famous passage, wrote of Methodism producing ' a new philanthropy which reformed our prisons, infused clemency and wisdom into our penal laws, abolished the slave trade, and gave the first impulses to popular education '. Wesley would have rejoiced as much as any man in these humanitarian results, but he would have been prompt to claim that it was all the product, and the inevitable product, of spiritual religion in the first place, and that there is no real love of our fellows that does not ultimately spring from the love of God, shed abroad in our hearts by the Holy Spirit. He wrote again and again of the love of God and the love of man, inseparably allied, as the source of all right actions, and the impulse that leads to the discharge of every social duty, and constrains us to ' do all possible good, of every possible kind, to all men '.

While the humanizing influence of the Evangelical Revival upon social life has been generously recognized, on the whole, there have been those on the other hand who have suggested that the revival delayed social progress by making men content with evil conditions in this world, because

they had the promise of heavenly bliss hereafter.
It would be difficult to find any evidence of this in
the lives of the early Methodists, or in the history
of the time. Wesley, at any rate, was always ready
to denounce social injustice wherever he saw it,
and in so far as there is any truth at all in the
notion of religion being an anodyne it is not so
much that it actually became so in fact, as that it
was suggested in such a capacity by the pious
platitudes of reactionary politicians. It was not
Wesley, but Burke, who said that the deserts of the
poor would be adjusted in ' the final proportions of
eternal justice '.

The general attitude of Wesley to social questions
might be said to be that of a shrewd man who was
an earnest Christian and also a man of his century.
He had no social theories of an original or revolutionary kind to propound, and he possessed no
supernatural prevision of the social developments
of the next century, and it is unfair to expect either
one or the other. It has been remarked that he
makes no comment in his *Journal* on the beginnings
of the French Revolution in 1789, but it ought to
be remembered that he was eighty-six years of age,
and still busy with the great work of his life. He
makes a few references to Rousseau, but never, I
think, to the Frenchman's views on social or
political matters.

There was much need for political reform in
Wesley's days, and in many directions, from the
House of Commons downward. The parliamentary
reforms which had been effected by the Long Parliament had all disappeared at the Restoration, and
the legislature was far from being really representative of the nation. Considerable towns like Birmingham and Manchester were entirely unrepre-
sented, while places that had decayed, and even

disappeared, still returned members to Parliament. Only about one person out of every fifty of the population of England was possessed of the franchise at all. It is interesting to note that Wesley was alive to these abuses, and was quite definitely in favour of measures of parliamentary reform. He wrote in 1754, ' I walked to Old Sarum, which, in spite of common sense, without house or inhabitant, still sends two members to the Parliament '. The next year he returns to the theme : ' I rode over the mountains, close to the sea, to Looe, a town near half as large as Islington, which sends four members to the Parliament ! And each county in North Wales sends one ! ' There does not seem to have been any particular agitation at the time to direct Wesley's attention to the subject. The younger Pitt made a fruitless attempt in 1782 to extinguish a group of rotten boroughs, and a plan of reform had been in his father's mind years before that, but the issue was not particularly in the air in 1754 and 1755, so far as I know. It was simply the circumstance of his visits to Old Sarum and Looe, notorious examples of farcical representation in Parliament, that suggested Wesley's remarks.

Wesley seems to have written nothing of much note upon political issues until late in life, and the occasion of his first political pamphlet was the agitation which gathered around the notorious John Wilkes, about the year 1770. Wilkes was a man of very profligate character in his personal life : it is curious to remember that his wife, who had much to endure from him, was a Methodist, and a member of one of the Societies in London. In his journal, the *North Briton* (so called in opposition to Smollett's paper, the *Briton*, with a derisive glance at his Scottish origin), Wilkes had denounced Bute, the Cabinet, and the Peace of Paris with great bitterness, and had largely brought about Bute's fall. Grenville succeeded Bute in 1763, and when Wilkes, in the forty-fifth number of the *North Briton*, strongly criticized the speech from the throne, and characterized a passage in it as ' the most abandoned instance of ministerial effrontery ever attempted to be imposed on mankind ', Grenville had a general warrant issued against the authors, printers, and publishers of the journal on a charge of seditious libel. Wilkes was sent to the Tower, and about fifty other persons were arrested. The arrest of Wilkes was flagrantly illegal, and he was released by the Court of Common Pleas, but he was immediately prosecuted for libel. While the case was still before the courts Parliament condemned Wilkes's utterance as a scandalous and seditious libel. Wilkes fled to France, and in 1764 was expelled from the House of Commons. In pursuance of his policy of repression, Grenville issued some two hundred injunctions against various public journals. The result of all this was a storm of indignation throughout the country, and a universal cry of ' Wilkes and Liberty ' !

Then in 1768 Wilkes returned to England and was imprisoned. Riots broke out all over the country during the next few months. The Government called out soldiers to disperse the mobs, and several rioters were killed. In 1769 the House of Commons again expelled Wilkes, but he was returned once more by an enormous majority. This was the occasion that produced the famous ' Letters of Junius ', which appeared in the *Public Advertiser* in 1769 – one of the most virulent and damaging attacks ever made upon a Government by way of the Press. It is interesting to remember that John Hampson, who had special sources of information, stated that, when the 'Letters of Junius' appeared, Wesley offered his services to the Government to answer them, and said, ' I will show the difference between rhetoric and logic '.[1]

Wesley published a tract, *Thoughts upon Liberty*, in 1772. This was called forth by the recent agitation connected with the prosecution of Wilkes, the riots in London, and the publication of the 'Letters of Junius '. Wesley's pamphlet is a defence of civil and religious liberty, and a confident statement that the English people possessed it ' in such a degree as was never known before, not from the times of William the Conqueror '. A note is appended to this last sentence : ' If the famous Middlesex election was an exception to this, yet observe, one swallow makes no summer.'

In the same year, 1772, Wesley published a tract entitled *Thoughts concerning the Origin of Power*. It is simply an attempt to refute the notion ' generally espoused by men of understanding and education, and that (if I do not mistake) not in England alone, but almost in every civilized nation ', that ' power must be originally derived from the people, and presupposes an original compact between them and their first governors '. He asks, ' Who are the people ? Are they every man, woman, and child ? ' and points out that women and men under age have no share in the choice of rulers. So that ' half the human species have been deprived of their natural right for want of a beard ', and ' myriads more for want of a stiff beard ', and so on. His conclusion is that power derives from God, but he does not specify in what way it is bestowed upon those who rule. He remarks caustically that the only instance he can recall where the people conferred power upon a ruler was that of Masaniello

[1] Hampson, *Life of Wesley*, III, p. 160.

in Naples in 1647, and adds, ' I apprehend that no
one desires that the people should take the same
steps in London '.

The eighteenth century was a period when there
was rather a special distrust of popular movements
that might easily lead to mob violence. And the
Methodists had particularly good reason to fear the
mob, for the life of Wesley and of almost every early
Methodist preacher had often been in danger at
the hands of enraged crowds. It is all the more
striking, therefore, that Wesley on more than one
occasion showed some sympathy with popular
demonstrations against low wages and high prices.
In 1758 he commended the action of the mob at
Sligo, though they had taken the law into their own
hands. ' Their business was only with the fore-
stallers of the market, who had bought up all the
corn far and near to starve the poor, and load a
Dutch ship, which lay at the quay ; but the mob
brought it all out into the market, and sold it for
the owners at the common price. And this they
did with all the calmness and composure imagin-
able, and without striking or hurting any one.' It
is quite evident, too, that Wesley did not dis-
approve of the action of the tinners at Truro in
1789, when he relates that ' a huge multitude, being
nearly starved, were come to beg or demand an
increase of their wages without which they could
not live '.

In the year 1773 Wesley wrote another pamphlet,
Thoughts on the Present Scarcity of Provisions. He
describes the great straits of the common people,
and then searches for the cause of the scarcity of
food, and selects as the main sources of the trouble
the great quantities of corn used in the distilleries,
' converting it into deadly poison ' ; the numbers
of horses kept for chaises and coaches, and the

number bred for export, which meant a larger consumption of oats, and a less production of oxen and
sheep ; the disappearance of small farms, with the
result that the farmers on a large scale did not
bother to produce pork, fowls, and eggs for the
markets, as the small farmers had previously done ;
the raising of agricultural rents ; and the increase
in the national taxes.

The reference to distilling in the last quotation is
enough to remind us that Wesley and the early
Methodists were pioneers in the temperance movement. That movement did not exist in the eighteenth century, of course, in the form it assumed
later. The early Methodists probably drank home-
brewed ale with their meals, as everybody else did
in those days. But Wesley always insisted upon the
strictest temperance in the use of alcoholic liquors,
and did his best to forbid the use of spirits altogether. In a letter to one of his followers in Ireland
Wesley wrote, ' Touch no dram. It is liquid fire.
It is a sure, though slow, poison. It saps the very
springs of life. In Ireland, above all countries in
the world, I would sacredly abstain from this,
because the evil is so general '.[1] In *A Farther Appeal
to Men of Reason and Religion* there is an impassioned
paragraph on the evil of drunkenness. ' Nor indeed
have our drunkards need to continue from morning
to night, until wine inflame them (the reference is
to Isaiah v. 11), seeing they have found a far more
compendious method of casting aside all sense and
reason, and disencumbering themselves of all remains either of conscience or of understanding.
So that whatever work of darkness is speedily to
be done, and that without danger of being interrupted either by fear, compassion, or remorse, they
may be in a few moments, by one draught, as

[1] Wesley's *Works*, XII, p. 233.

effectually qualified for it, as if they could swallow a legion of devils ! '[1]   In the sermon on ' The Use of Money ' Wesley writes of ' that liquid fire, commonly called drams, or spirituous liquors.   It is true, these may have a place in medicine : they may be of use in some bodily disorders, although there would rarely be occasion for them, were it not for the unskilfulness of the practitioner.   Therefore such as prepare and sell them only for this end may keep their consciences clear.   But who are they ? Who prepare them only for this end ?   Do you know ten such distillers in England ?   Then excuse these.   But all who sell them in the common way, to any that will buy, are poisoners general.   They murder His Majesty's subjects by wholesale, neither does their eye pity or spare '.[2]

Wesley wrote a series of brief tracts, only a couple of pages or so in length, intended to be given away as occasion arose, and entitled *A Word to a Smuggler*, *A Word to a Swearer*, *A Word to an Unhappy Woman*, and so on.   One of the most passionate and pungent of these is *A Word to a Drunkard*.   It begins, ' Are you a man ?   God made you a man, but you make yourself a beast . . . a mere beast, not a fool, not a madman only, but a swine, a poor, filthy swine. Go and wallow with them in the mire ! '

Wesley made many references to war, and always denounced it as a madness and a barbarity, but he never plainly adopted the position of thoroughgoing pacifism, as indeed no one else did in his days, except (to their everlasting honour be it said) the Society of Friends.   In a letter to Thomas Rankin, Wesley wrote : ' When a land is visited with famine, or plague, or earthquake, the people commonly see and acknowledge the hand of God. *But wherever war breaks out, God is forgotten*, if He be

[1] Wesley's *Works*, VIII, p. 162.   [2] Wesley's *Works*, VI, pp. 128–9.

not set at open defiance. What a glorious work of
God was at Cambuslang and Kilsyth, from 1740
to 1744 ! But the war that followed tore it all up
by the roots, and left scarce any trace of it behind ;
insomuch that when I diligently inquired a few
years after, I could not find one that retained the
life of God ! '[1]   In his sermon on ' National Sins
and Miseries ' he writes : ' And, as if all this were
not misery enough, see likewise the fell monster,
war !   But who can describe the complicated
misery which is contained in this ?   Hark ! the
cannon's roar !   A pitchy cloud covers the face of
the sky.   Noise, confusion, terror, reign over all !
Dying groans are on every side.   The bodies of men
are pierced, torn, hewed in pieces :   their blood is
poured out on the earth like water.'[2]

In his treatise on *The Doctrine of Original Sin*
Wesley wrote : ' There is a still more horrid re-
proach to the Christian name, yea to the name of
man, to all reason and humanity.   There is war in
the world !   war between men !   war between
Christians !   I mean, between those that bear the
name of Christ, and profess to " walk as He also
walked ".   Now, who can reconcile war, I will not
say to religion, but to any degree of reason or common sense ? '[3]   On a later page of the same work
there is a passage which resembles rather curiously
a striking paragraph in Carlyle's *Sartor Resartus* :
' But, whatever be the cause, let us calmly and im-
partially consider the thing itself.   Here are forty
thousand men gathered together on this plain.
What are they going to do ?   See, there are thirty
or forty thousand more at a little distance.   And
these are going to shoot them through the head or
body, to stab them, or split their skulls, and send

---

[1] Wesley's *Works*, XII, p. 311.   [2] Wesley's *Works*, IX, p. 221.
[3] Wesley's *Works*, VII, p. 404.

most of their souls into everlasting fire, as fast as
they possibly can. Why so ? What harm have
they done to them ? O, none at all ! They do not
so much as know them. But a man, who is King
of France, has a quarrel with another man, who is
King of England. So these Frenchmen are to kill
as many of these Englishmen as they can, to prove
the King of France is in the right. Now, what an
argument is this ! What a method of proof ! What
an amazing way of deciding controversies ! What
must mankind be, before such a thing as war could
ever be known or thought of upon earth ? How
shocking, how inconceivable a want must there
have been of common understanding, as well as
common humanity, before any two Governors, or
any two nations in the universe, could once think
of such a method of decision ! If, then, all nations,
Pagan, Mahometan, and Christian, do, in fact,
make this their last resort, what farther proof do
we need of the utter degeneracy of all nations from
the plainest principles of reason and virtue ? of the
absolute want, both of common sense and common
humanity, which runs through the whole race of
mankind ? '[1] In *A Seasonable Address to the More
Serious Part of the Inhabitants of Great Britain respecting
the Unhappy Contest between Us and our American
Brethren*, which appeared in 1776, there is a similar
passage, but it is quoted from some unnamed
writer. ' See ! Here are some thousands of our
brave countrymen gathered together on this plain :
they are followed by the most tender and feeling
emotions of wives, children, and an innumerable
multitude of their thoughtful, humane, and sym-
pathizing countrymen. Then turn your eyes and
behold a superior number at a little distance, of
their brethren, " flesh of their flesh, and bone of

[1] Wesley's *Works*, IX, p. 222.

their bone ", who only a few years since emigrated
to the dreary wilds of America. These also are
followed with the most tender feelings of wives,
children, and countrymen. See, they advance towards each other, well prepared with every instrument of death ! But what are they going to do ?
To shoot each other through the head or heart ;
to stab and butcher each other, and hasten (it is to
be feared) one another into the everlasting burn-
ings. Why so ? What harm have they done to
one another ? Why, none at all. Most of them are
entire strangers to each other. But a matter is in
dispute relative to the mode of taxation. So these
countrymen, children of the same parents, are to
murder each other with all possible haste, to prove
who is in the right. Now, what an argument is this !
What a method of proof ! What an amazing way
of deciding controversies ! But so it is ; and O
what horrors attend on it ! At what a price is the
decision made ! By the blood and wounds of
thousands ; the burning cities, ravaging and laying
waste the country.'[1]

The most famous intervention of Wesley in
political affairs, as this last passage may remind us,
was in relation to the troubles in America. He had
a special interest in America, both because of his
own early sojourn in Georgia, and because of the
growth of Methodism in the colonies. At first his
sympathies were clearly with the colonists in their
protest against their grievances. In his pamphlet,
Free Thoughts on the State of Public Affairs, he wrote,
' I do not defend the measures which have been
taken with regard to America : I doubt whether
any man can defend them either on the foot of law,
equity, or prudence '. In June 1775, at the very
time when the war was beginning, he wrote to Lord

[1] Wesley's *Works*, XI, p. 121.

North, the Prime Minister, ' In spite of all my long-
rooted prejudices, I cannot avoid thinking, if I think
at all, these, an oppressed people, asked for nothing
more than their legal rights, and that in the most
modest and inoffensive manner that the nature of
the thing would allow. But, waiving this, waiving
all considerations of right and wrong, I ask, Is it
common sense to use force against the Americans ? '
He goes on to warn the statesman that the revolting
colonists are ' terribly united ', and that ' they will
probably dispute every inch of ground and if they
die, die sword in hand ', and finishes with a passionate appeal, ' Remember Rehoboam ! Remember Philip the Second ! Remember Charles the
First ! '   There is an almost prophetic quality in
this ; as Tyerman points out, the battle of Bunker's
Hill was fought within a couple of days of Wesley's
writing the letter. Four months later, in a letter
to John Rankin, one of his preachers, he states that
if he has an interview, which seems to be not unlikely, with ' a great man ' – probably either Lord
North or Lord Dartmouth[1] – he will urge upon
him, ' without any circumlocution ', that ' love and
tender measures will do far more than violence '.[2]

Then appears a most astonishing change in
Wesley's attitude. In the autumn of 1775 he published a tract entitled *A Calm Address to our American
Colonies*. The position that taxation implies the
right to representation, he argues, is one that has
never been recognized in England, and the colonists

[1] Lord Dartmouth, who was Secretary for the Colonies, was a Methodist.
His seat was Sandwell Hall, near Birmingham, and when in residence there
he used to ride over to Wednesbury to meet in his Society Class. Cowper
has a reference to him in *Truth* :

    ' We boast some great ones whom the Gospel sways,
      And one who wears a coronet and prays.'

[2] Tyerman, *Life of Wesley*, III, p. 197.

have all the rights that Englishmen possess, except those they have necessarily surrendered by leaving the mother country !

Wesley admitted that this tract represented a complete change of attitude, and he defended himself by pleading that he had read Dr. Johnson's *Taxation no Tyranny*, and it had altered his views. As a matter of fact, his own tract is simply Johnson's, shortened and simplified. Whether he had Johnson's permission to do this or not, Johnson did not object. He wrote to Wesley, and said, ' I have thanks to return for the addition of your important suffrage to my argument on the American question. To have gained such a mind as yours may justly confirm me in my own opinion. What effect my paper has had upon the public I know not ; but I have no reason to be discouraged. The lecturer was surely in the right who though he saw his audience slinking away refused to quit the chair while Plato stayed ' – as graceful a compliment as Johnson (who could be polite when he liked) ever paid to any one.

There are some indications, I think, that Wesley was not very comfortable in his own mind as to his pamphlet. In the *Journal*, on November 11, 1775, he wrote : ' I made some additions to the *Calm Address to our American Colonies*. Need any one ask from what motive this was wrote ? Let him look round ; England is in a flame ! A flame of malice and rage against the King, and almost all that are in authority under him. I labour to put out this flame. Ought not every true patriot to do the same ? If hireling writers on either side judge of me by themselves, that I cannot help.' This sounds like rather an uneasy defence.

The question of religious toleration came into prominence about 1780, and occasioned some expressions of opinion by Wesley on the subject.   His position was perfectly clear, and perfectly logical. In a letter to the *Public Advertiser* in 1780 relating to the current controversies – it was the period of Sir George Savile's measure for the relief of Roman Catholics, and the ensuing riots associated with the name of Lord George Gordon – he writes, ' With persecution I have nothing to do.   I persecute no man for his religious principles.   Let there be as boundless a freedom in religion as any man can conceive '.   But he goes on to argue that the Roman Catholic principle that no faith is to be kept with heretics makes it unsafe for any Protestant country to give to Roman Catholics the fullest privileges of civil liberty, because whatever oaths of loyalty they take may be disavowed.   ' The Romanists never have been persecuted in England since I remember. They have enjoyed a full toleration.   I wish them to enjoy the same toleration still ;   neither more nor less.   I would not hurt a hair of their head.   Meantime I would not put it into their power to hurt me, or any other person whom they believe to be heretics.   I steer the middle way.   I would neither kill nor be killed.   I would not use the sword against them, nor put it into their hands lest they should use it against me ;   I wish them well, but I dare not trust them.'[1]   This is a logical conclusion which (however it may be assailed from the Catholic side) is difficult to demolish, at least until the Roman Catholic Church has authoritatively disavowed its established principles – that it has the right to break faith with heretics, and to punish them.   We must remember, too, that there had been a good deal of persecution of Protestants on the Continent during Wesley's lifetime, and there was a genuine fear, and not at all an unreasonable one, that if the Roman

[1] Wesley's *Works*, X, pp. 174–5.

Catholics got the upper hand in England the same thing would happen here.

Much of the social and political reform that was ultimately due, in a large measure, to the influence of Methodism, was actually brought into effect by the evangelical party in the Established Church and in Dissent, rather than by the Methodists themselves. This introduces a curious and rather complicated set of facts. Wesley's own followers were generally of humble rank and moderate means, while it was only wealthy people who could establish large philanthropies, and it was only people of some social standing who could influence projects of social or political reform where legislative action was needed. Now, as far as Methodism had any direct influence upon the upper classes and the rich it was mainly through Whitefield, and not through Wesley – rather a singular fact, when one remembers that Wesley had aristocratic family connexions, while Whitefield was the son of an innkeeper at Gloucester. But Whitefield was a wonderful orator, and his preaching attracted the attention of Selina, Countess of Huntingdon, who finally made him her domestic chaplain. She brought Whitefield to the knowledge of a host of her acquaintances, and Frederick, Prince of Wales, the Duke of Cumberland, Lord Bolingbroke, Lord Chesterfield, Lord Lyttelton, Lord North, Lord Sandwich, Lord Townshend, Bubb Dodington, William Pitt, George Selwyn, and Horace Walpole, were all found in his congregations. Walpole wrote to Horace Mann at Florence, ' If you think of coming to England, you must prepare yourself with Methodism. I really think by that time it will be necessary '. A great many titled ladies were also found in Whitefield's congregations. The Duchess of Ancaster, the Duchess of Buckingham, the

Duchess of Marlborough, and the Duchess of Queensberry – Prior's ' Kitty, beautiful and young, And wild as colt untam'd ' – Lady Cobham, Lady Frankland, Lady Hinchinbrooke, Lady Lisburne, and Lady Townshend, were all among Whitefield's hearers, at one time or another, though some of these ladies seem to have been far enough from any real experience of religion – the Duchess of Buckingham, for example, said that the doctrines of the Methodist preachers were ' most repulsive, and strongly tinctured with impertinence and disrespect toward their superiors. . . . It is monstrous to be told that you have a heart as sinful as the common wretches that crawl on the earth. This is highly offensive and insulting '. This self-satisfied dame was the bastard daughter of James the Second, and the divorced wife of the Earl of Anglesey. Her second husband was the Duke of Buckingham, and she died in his town house (now Buckingham Palace) in 1742.

Whitefield had a naïve delight in recording the number of aristocratic folk who came to hear him preach. There is a curious contrast between him and Wesley in this respect, for Wesley had a frank contempt for the intelligence of such people. He seldom preached to ' a genteel audience ' without adding some caustic comment in his *Journal* like this : ' Observing some lords and ladies in my congregation, I endeavoured to reduce my discourse to the level of their understanding ' ; or this, ' O how hard it is to be shallow enough for a polite audience ! ' But Whitefield, as we have said, exercised a considerable influence for good upon people of high social position, and this influence passed, to some extent, and in one direction, into the Evangelical party in the Established Church and the activities of the Clapham Sect.

Then some of Wesley's sympathizers and helpers
from the early days were Anglican clergymen, like
Whitefield himself, Fletcher, Dr. Coke, William
Grimshaw, the Curate of Haworth, and Vincent
Perronet, the Vicar of Shoreham. The association
of others with Wesley was less close, but men like
William Romaine in London, John Beveridge at
Everton, Samuel Walker at Truro, Henry Venn at
Huddersfield, Rowland Hill at Surrey Chapel,
Martin Madan at the Lock Hospital, were all pro-
ducts of the Evangelical Revival, and except for the
Calvinism of some of them, and their acceptance of
the parish system and the ecclesiastical order of the
Church of England generally, they preached and
ministered in a way that was very like that of
Wesley's preachers. One or two others have some
special importance because of literary or personal
connexions. John Newton, after a wild and
debauched career as a sailor, was wonderfully converted, and became Curate of Olney and later
Rector of St. Mary Woolnoth in London. While
at Olney he was friendly with Cowper, and (despite
all that has been ignorantly written on the subject)
exercised a thoroughly healthy influence on the
unhappy poet. The Olney hymns were written
by this oddly assorted pair, and, strange as it seems,
the very best of the hymns were not written by the
poet, but by Newton. Thomas Scott, who was
much influenced by Newton, wrote a *Commentary*
that was once widely popular, and also a devotional
book entitled *The Force of Truth*. Newman confessed, in the *Apologia pro vita Sua*, how much he
owed to the writings of Scott – ' the writer who
made a deeper impression on my mind than any
other, and to whom (humanly speaking) I almost
owe my soul – Thomas Scott of Aston Sandford. I
so admired and delighted in his writings, that, when

I was an undergraduate, I thought of making a visit to his Parsonage, in order to see a man whom I so deeply revered. I hardly think I could have given up the idea of this expedition, even after I had taken my degree ; for the news of his death in 1821 came upon me as a disappointment as well as a sorrow. I hung upon the lips of Daniel Wilson, afterwards Bishop of Calcutta, as in two sermons at St. John's Chapel he gave the history of Scott's life and death. I had been possessed of his *Force of Truth* and *Essays* from a boy ; his *Commentary* I bought when I was an undergraduate. What, I suppose, will strike any reader of Scott's history and writings is his bold unworldliness and vigorous independence of mind '. It is a great testimony to Scott's work and character that men so widely different as Newman and Carey should have been profoundly influenced for good by him. For Carey, the famous missionary (and the founder of the Baptist Missionary Society), when he was a shoe-maker in the neighbourhood of Olney, came under Scott's influence and said, later, ' If I know any-thing of the work of God in my soul, I owe it to the preaching of Mr. Scott '. Scott himself was one of the founders of the Church Missionary Society.

In the next generation there were two main centres of the evangelical movement within the Established Church. One was Cambridge, where Charles Simeon at Holy Trinity had a far-reaching influence upon the life of the University. The other was Clapham, where several evangelical laymen happened to live, and where, in consequence, the leading evangelicals used frequently to meet. These excellent people were labelled by Sydney Smith ' the Clapham Sect '. William Wilberforce, John Thornton, Zachary Macaulay, Granville Sharp, and Thomas Clarkson, were leading members of the

group.   Wilberforce was M.P. for York, and a
friend of the younger Pitt.   Granville Sharp and
Thomas Clarkson were closely associated with him
in his fight for the abolition of the slave trade.
John Thornton was practically the founder of the
British and Foreign Bible Society.   He was an
exceedingly generous supporter of every religious
and philanthropic cause : he must have given away
in the course of his life hundreds of thousands of
pounds.   Cowper said of him that he had

> an industry in doing good
> Restless as his who toils and sweats for food.

It was Thornton, by the way, who presented Newton
to the rectory of St. Mary Woolnoth.   Zachary
Macaulay was active in all these good works, and
is also remembered as the father of the famous
historian and essayist.

Two of the earliest Methodists to enter Parliament, Joseph Butterworth, M.P. for Coventry and
later for Dover, and Thomas Thompson, M.P. for
Midhurst, were associated with the Clapham
evangelicals in their reforming efforts, and Dr.
Thomas Coke and Dr. Adam Clarke, two of Wesley's preachers, were also in fairly close touch with
the group.

It was very largely this group of Evangelicals,
more or less within the Established Church, that
led the way in philanthropic efforts of various
kinds, such as prison reform and the abolition of
the slave trade, as well as in more directly religious
efforts, such as foreign missions.   In all these things
they had behind them the solid and enthusiastic
support of Wesley's followers, but most of the
Methodists, properly so called, had neither the
wealth nor the social and political influence which

would have enabled them to take the lead in the way that men like Wilberforce and Thornton did. But it must not be forgotten that the men of this group ultimately owed all their inspiration to Methodism.

Methodism had a very special interest in prison reform, for one of the very earliest activities of the original group of Methodists had been the visiting of prisons. Wesley had himself engaged in this work while he was at Oxford. Later in life he visited the jails and preached to the prisoners on hundreds of occasions. In one period of nine months Wesley preached more than sixty times in various prisons. As we have seen, one of the early preachers, Silas Told, devoted his apostolic life expressly to the welfare of the prisoners in the jails of London. Wesley maintained a keen interest in the matter all his life. On January 2, 1761, he wrote to the *London Chronicle* : ' Of all the seats of woe on this side hell, few, I suppose, exceed or even equal Newgate. If any region of horror could exceed it a few years ago, Newgate in Bristol did ; so great was the filth, the stench, the misery, and wickedness, which shocked all who had a spark of humanity left. How was I surprised, then, when I was there a few weeks ago ! . . . And does not the keeper of Newgate deserve to be remembered full as well as the Man of Ross ? May the Lord remember him on that day ! Meanwhile, will no one follow his example ? ' On the occasion of the visit to which Wesley refers, in the previous October, he records in his *Journal* that he ' preached a charity sermon in Newgate for the use of the poor prisoners ', and then appends a long description of the reformed state of the jail. We know what prisons were like in the eighteenth century, but if we did not we could soon find out, by merely picturing the state of things in the absence of the very elementary decencies that Wesley describes and praises. He notes that the prison is thoroughly cleansed twice a week ; that there is no brawling and fighting ; that there is no drunkenness, ' however advantageous it might be to the keeper and the tapster ' ; that the women are kept apart from the men, and that prostitutes are not allowed to visit the prison, ' no, not at any price ' ; that those who are willing to work at their trades are allowed to do so ; and that the sick are given medical attention.

John Howard began to investigate the condition of the prisons in 1773, when he was appointed (although a Dissenter) High Sheriff of Bedfordshire. His book on *The State of the Prisons in England and Wales* was not published until 1777, but before this, in 1774, there had been two Acts of Parliament with which he had to do, dealing with some of the particular abuses, especially the fees paid to jailers, and the insanitary state of the prisons – a fact which shows that the public conscience was at last being roused in the matter. But Wesley, as we have seen, tried to rouse it many years before.

Wesley had some personal acquaintance with Howard, and held him in high honour, and Howard, on his part, acknowledged that Wesley had helped to inspire him in his campaign for the reform of the prisons. On June 28, 1787, Wesley writes in his *Journal* : ' I had the pleasure of a conversation with Mr. Howard, I think one of the greatest men in Europe. Nothing but the mighty power of God can enable him to go through his difficult and dangerous employments. But what can hurt us, if God is on our side ? ' In a letter to Walter Churchey on June 20, 1789, there is a later reference to the philanthropist. ' Mr. Howard is really an extraordinary man. God has raised him up to be a blessing to many nations. I do not doubt, but there has been something more than natural in his preservation hitherto, and should not wonder if the providence of God should hereafter be still more conspicuous in his favour.'

In the account he wrote of a meeting with Wesley at Dublin in 1787 Howard says : ' I was encouraged by him to go on vigorously with my own designs. I saw in him how much a single man might achieve by zeal and perseverance ; and I thought, why may I not do as much in my way as Mr. Wesley has done in his, if I am only as assiduous and persevering ? and I determined I would pursue my work with more alacrity than ever.' It is evident that Howard found a quite exceptional stimulus in Wesley's encouragement, and in his example. On the eve of Howard's last expedition he sought another interview with Wesley, and went to City Road for the purpose, but the restless old evangelist was on his way to Ireland and the two never met again.

Howard's interest in prisons and prison reform was probably first stirred when as a young man, on a voyage to Lisbon, the vessel on which he sailed was captured by a French privateer, and he spent some time in a French prison. It is interesting to note Wesley's interest in the Frenchmen who were prisoners in England. On October 15, 1759, Wesley writes : ' I walked up to Knowle, a mile from Bristol, to see the French prisoners. Above eleven hundred of them, we were informed, were confined in that little place, without anything to lie on but a little dirty straw, or anything to cover them but a few foul thin rags, either by day or night, so that they died like rotten sheep. I was much affected, and preached in the evening on, (Exodus xxiii. 9,) " Thou shalt not oppress a stranger ; for ye know the heart of a stranger, seeing ye were strangers in the land of Egypt ". Eighteen pounds were contributed immediately, which were made up to four-and-twenty the next day. With this we bought linen and woollen cloth, which were made up into shirts, waistcoats, and breeches. Some dozen of stockings were added ; all of which were carefully distributed, where there was the greatest want. Presently after, the Corporation of Bristol sent a large quantity of mattresses and blankets. And it was not long before contributions were set on foot at London, and in various parts of the kingdom ; so that I believe from this time they were pretty well provided with all the necessities of life.'

The abolition of slavery is as closely associated with the name of Wilberforce as that of prison reform is with the name of Howard. Wilberforce and several of his helpers belonged to the Evangelical party, and they had behind them the solid and enthusiastic support of practically all the Dissenters, and especially of the Quakers and the Methodists. The cause began to attract a good deal of public attention after 1772, when Granville Sharp won the Somersett case. Thomas Clarkson wrote his Latin prize essay on slavery at Oxford in 1785,[1] and soon after began to agitate on the subject – ' starting in his fervent prime, He first led forth that enterprise sublime ', as Wordsworth said in the rather pedestrian sonnet he addressed to Clarkson in 1807. Clarkson persuaded Wilberforce to take up the cause in Parliament, and a committee, of which Sharp was president, was formed in 1787. It is interesting to note that the ' Resolutions of the Society for the Purpose of effecting the Abolition of the Slave Trade ' were printed in the

---

[1] On the question *anne liceat invitos in servitutem dare ?*

Arminian Magazine in 1788. Clarkson has recorded that, when the committee was formed, a letter of warm encouragement from Wesley was received, in which he promised to issue a large new edition of his *Thoughts on Slavery*, to which he would add a commendation of their design. In October 1787 another letter was received from Wesley giving some shrewd advice as to procedure, and assuring the members of the committee that he took, if possible, a still deeper interest ' in their glorious concern'. Many years of work and of disappointment followed after this ; the Act of Parliament which abolished the slave trade was not passed until March 1807, and slavery in the British dominions was not finally abolished until 1833.

Wesley's interest in the abolition of slavery began long before the period of the agitation, however. He records that on February 11, 1772, he read Sterne's *Sentimental Journey*, and expresses a very poor opinion of it. The next day he writes : ' In returning, I read a very different book, published by an honest Quaker, on that execrable sum of all villainies, commonly called the Slave Trade. I read of nothing like it in the heathen world, whether ancient or modern ; And it infinitely exceeds, in every instance of barbarity, whatever Christian slaves suffer in Mahometan countries.' The ' honest Quaker ' was Anthony Benezet, and the book was either *A Caution and Warning to Great Britain and her Colonies on the Calamitous State of the Enslaved Negroes* (1767) or *Some Account of Guinea, with an Enquiry into the Slave Trade* (1771) – probably the former. It was the reading of these books, by the way, that led Clarkson to write his Oxford dissertation and to become interested in the abolition of slavery.

Wesley's pamphlet *Thoughts on Slavery*, to which

reference has been made, was issued in 1774. It is one of the most damning attacks upon slavery that had ever been made up to that time, and must have exercised an enormous influence upon the large public that Wesley commanded. It is written with intense conviction and feeling, for Wesley had seen the horrors of slavery in America. ' One gentleman, when I was abroad,' he remarks, ' thought fit to roast his slave alive.' The tract ends with the impassioned words, ' O Thou God of love, Thou who art loving to every man, and whose mercy is over all Thy works ; Thou who art the Father of the spirits of all flesh, and who art rich in mercy unto all ; Thou who hast mingled of one blood all the nations upon earth ; have compassion upon these outcasts of men, who are trodden down as dung upon the earth ! Arise, and help those who have no helper, whose blood is spilt upon the ground like water ! Are not these also the work of Thine own hands, the purchase of Thy Son's blood ? stir them up to cry unto Thee in the land of their captivity ; and let their complaint come up before Thee ; let it enter into Thine ears ! '

It is interesting to remember that Wilberforce, among his many charitable deeds, paid a pension to the widow of Charles Wesley. Hannah More had introduced Wilberforce and Charles Wesley to each other years before, but John Wesley does not appear to have met the liberator until February 24, 1789, when he writes in his *Journal*, ' Mr. Wilberforce called upon me, and we had an agreeable and useful conversation. What a blessing is it to Mr. Pitt to have such a friend as this ! ' Wilberforce's account of the visit is more succinct : ' I called on John Wesley, a fine old fellow.'

Four days before his death, on February 24, 1791, Wesley wrote a famous letter to Wilberforce,

encouraging him in his crusade against slavery :
' Unless the divine power has raised you up to be
as *Athanasius contra mundum*, I see not how you can
go through your glorious enterprise, in opposing
that execrable villainy, which is the scandal of
religion, of England, and of human nature. Unless
God has raised you up for this very thing, you will
be worn out by the opposition of men and devils.
But, if God be for you, who can be against you ?
Are all of them together stronger than God ? O
be not weary in well doing ! Go on, in the name
of God and in the power of His might, till even
American slavery (the vilest that ever saw the sun)
shall vanish away before it.

' Reading this morning a tract, wrote by a poor
African, I was particularly struck by that circumstance that a man who has a black skin, being
wronged or outraged by a white man, can have no
redress ; it being a law, in all our colonies, that the
oath of a black against a white goes for nothing.
What villainy is this !

' That He who has guided you from your youth
up, may continue to strengthen you in this and in
all things, is the prayer of, Dear Sir, Your affec-
tionate servant, John Wesley.'[1]

There is an astonishing contrast between Wesley
and Whitefield in this matter. Whitefield definitely
advocated slavery, and was actually a slave-owner.
He bequeathed fifty slaves to the Countess of Huntingdon, and she bought still more. It is true that
Whitefield died before the public conscience had
been roused in the matter of slavery, but, for all
that, his attitude is in melancholy contrast to that
of Wesley, who had been a consistent opponent of
slavery all his life. In his early days in Georgia the
settlers clamoured for the right to import slaves,

[1] Wesley's *Works*, XIII, pp. 127-8.

PM

and Whitefield sympathized with them, but Wesley stood by Oglethorpe and the Trustees in their policy of refusing to sanction slavery. It was allowed in South Carolina ; the Wesleys saw it there, and Charles Wesley denounced the cruelties of it when he returned to England.

Wesley was interested all his life in the question of Christian education. He was deeply dissatisfied with the state of things he had experienced both at the Charterhouse and at Oxford. He had taken note, also, of what he saw in the Pietist institutions at Halle and in the Moravian institutions at Herrn-hut. When Wesley was at Halle in 1738 he records, on July 24, that he went to see ' the Orphan House, that amazing proof that all things are still possible to him that believeth. There is now a large yearly revenue for its support, beside what is continually brought in by the printing-office, the books sold there, and the apothecary's shop, which is furnished with all sorts of medicines. . . . The lodging-chambers for the children, their dining-room, their chapel, and all the adjoining apartments, are so conveniently contrived, and so exactly clean, as I have never seen any before. Six hundred and fifty children, we were informed, are wholly maintained there ; and three thousand, if I mistake not, taught '. A little later, under the date August 10, Wesley gives an account of the Orphan House at Herrnhut, and remarks that the children rise at five and retire at ten ; that they go for a walk before and after dinner and after supper ; that they are taught writing, arithmetic, history, and French ; and that ' those who are capable of it learn Latin '.

It may be remarked here, in passing, that the apothecary's department at Halle probably suggested to Wesley one of his minor philanthropies.

The Methodists organized a free dispensary for the sick poor in London in 1746, and it did excellent work until 1754.   Moreover, in 1747 Wesley published *Primitive Physic, or An Easy and Natural Method of Curing Most Diseases*.   It went through twenty-three editions in Wesley's lifetime.   Some of the remedies are quaint, but the hygienic rules given are sensible, and undoubtedly the odd little book was very serviceable in practice.

The next Methodist building to be erected after the meeting-house at Bristol was the Orphan House at Newcastle, which retains the name, by the way, to this very day.   Wesley meant it to be on the model of Francke's Waisenhaus at Halle, but that design was never fulfilled.   Finally it became merely a preaching-place, with a residence for Wesley and his preachers attached.   But the title-deeds of the Orphan House make provision for a school with one master, one mistress, and forty poor children, and the school existed for some time.

Wesley also instituted a charity school at the Foundery in London, of which that very extraordinary man, Silas Told, was the first master. Wesley maintained an interest in it all his life, for on November 12, 1786, he writes : ' I preached, morning and afternoon, for the use of our little charity-school, where forty boys and twenty girls are trained up both for this world and the world to come.'   The school lasted into the nineteenth century, having been transferred to another site.

His next educational enterprise was the school at Kingswood.   The locality was no doubt chosen because it was one of first fields of Methodist work, but it was also in accordance with Wesley's conviction that such a school should not be in a large town, and yet should not be too far away from one. He held that the course of instruction in most schools was very defective ; especially that writing, arithmetic, and geography were neglected in order to make time for Latin and Greek, while neverthe-less the order in which the classics were read was often an entirely wrong one ; and that above all the spirit of religion was lacking in nearly all the schools.

Wesley had infinite trouble over Kingswood, and it is no wonder. His ideals of discipline were monastic in their strictness, and there is nothing in the whole of his life in which he shows to less advan-tage than here. His intentions were of the best, but he certainly did not understand the mind of childhood. He tried to introduce into the school all the Spartan rigour of his own early home, and forgot that in a school it could not be tempered by parental love, as it had been in the parsonage at Epworth. Kingswood has developed into one of the leading public schools of England, attended largely, but not exclusively, by the sons of Methodist ministers.

The establishment of Sunday schools is always connected with the name of Robert Raikes of Gloucester, and no doubt on general grounds the honour is rightly accredited. But the Methodists distinctly anticipated Raikes. As early as 1769 Hannah Ball, a Methodist of High Wycombe, had set up a regular school for children where they met every Sunday. It was another Methodist, Sophia Cooke (afterward the wife of Samuel Bradburn), who suggested the idea to Raikes.

Wesley recorded in his *Journal* that on July 18, 1784, he visited the Sunday school that had been recently established in connexion with the parish church at Bingley, and remarked, ' I find these schools springing up wherever I go. Perhaps God may have a deeper end therein than men are aware of. Who knows but some of these schools may become nurseries for Christians ? ' The next year,

1785, Wesley published in the *Arminian Magazine* a letter by Robert Raikes, ' An Account of the Sunday Charity Schools lately begun in various Parts of England '. Wesley, in fact, warmly supported the innovation, and the movement spread so rapidly that by 1787 there were two hundred thousand children in the Sunday schools.

It will be seen that Wesley's attitude to political and social reform was, for a man of his age and his antecedents, rather a liberal one, on the whole. But there can be no doubt at all that the temper of Methodism changed a good deal in this respect in the generation that followed his death. Some reasons for this are plain. The wild excesses of the French Revolution, and the anti-religious attitude of the Revolutionary leaders, undoubtedly had a very considerable effect in throwing the sympathies of peaceable and religious folk on to the side of reactionary politics. Probably the fact that many Methodists, through their honesty and industry in business, were becoming comparatively well-to-do, had some influence in the same direction. While the movement remained a popular one, and nine-tenths of the Methodists were still working folk, there were some of them who were acquiring a middle-class respectability, with its characteristic horror of anything that looked revolutionary.

It is curious, and rather disappointing, to contrast the attitude of the leaders of Methodism in the early nineteenth century with that of Wesley in the matter of parliamentary reform, for example. The massacre of Peterloo in 1819 roused all the liberal element in the nation to bitter wrath. A peaceful demonstration was held on St. Peter's Field in Manchester in favour of parliamentary reform. The magistrates were frightened out of their senses. A troop of yeomanry charged the crowd and a dozen people were killed. But the official attitude of Methodism at the time toward such demonstrations was merely to dissuade the members of the Societies from attending ' the tumultuous assemblies which have lately been witnessed in many parts of the country ', and to threaten those who did attend with expulsion.

Another incident of a rather later time shows much the same spirit. A number of Methodists at Tolpuddle, in Dorset, had formed a trade union in 1834. Their wages had been successively reduced from ten to seven shillings a week, and in their straits they first made some inquiries about the existing trade unions, and then established a Friendly Society of Agricultural Labourers. For this they were arrested, tried, and sentenced to seven years' transportation, and this monstrous abuse of justice was warmly approved by the Home Secretary in Parliament. A Methodist woman went up to London to interview Dr. Jabez Bunting on behalf of the victims. He would not, or, at least, he did not, see her. The ultimate release of the Tolpuddle pioneers was due to agitation by Radicals, and Methodists do not appear to have had any part in it.

But it should be remembered, on the other side, that many of the leaders of the trade union movement, from the earliest days down to the present, were Methodists, and that many more were trained in Methodism. It was here that they learned the elements of oratory, and the art of dealing with men, in their work as lay preachers and in other offices of the Church, and, what was vastly more important, it was here that they found first of all their unselfish idealism, and all the nobler impulses of service.

It is rather singular, and perhaps unfortunate,

that the Methodist people stood aloof to the extent they did from Chartism. There were Chartist leaders who had been Methodists, and probably the movement owed a great deal to Methodism in an indirect way. But the Methodist people generally were antagonized by the threats of violence, as well as by the professed infidelity of O'Connor and some others. The happenings in Paris in 1830 also had the effect of renewing amongst peaceable people the dread of revolution, which dated from the last years of the preceding century.

But however we excuse the conservative temper of the Methodist leaders, and, to a less extent, of the Methodist people, in the first half of the nineteenth century, it can hardly be denied that it was directly responsible for the worst disasters that ever befell Methodism – a calamitous series of secessions from which it has never really recovered to this day. For the very same spirit of political conservatism that made Methodists shy of Chartism, and of liberal movements in politics generally, became a spirit of ecclesiastical conservatism and clericalism within the Conference, and the repressive measures that were taken by the Conference made inevitable the series of disturbances and secessions that culminated in 1857.

It should be understood that the divisions of Methodism were not all actually secessions. A great evangelistic movement which began in Staffordshire in the early years of the nineteenth century, under the leadership of Hugh Bourne and William Clowes, brought the Primitive Methodists into existence, and a similar but far smaller movement in the West about the same period, under William O'Bryan and James Thorne, led to the formation of the community known as Bible Christians. These were not disruptions : they were new outbreaks of more or less independent evangelism, deriving from Methodism much as the Salvation Army did in a later day. But there was also a distinct movement within Methodism in the direction of more liberal and more popular ecclesiastical government, and, while there were no doubt faults on both sides, I cannot conceal my own conviction that the rigidity, and indeed the tyranny, of the Conference, which was in the very worst tradition of clerical autocracy, was mainly responsible for the disasters that came to pass. The Methodist New Connexion was formed in 1797, under the leadership of Alexander Kilham. The United Methodist Free Churches were formed in 1857. This community resulted from the amalgamation of one or two minor secessions of an earlier date with a large body of Reformers, led by James Everett, William Griffith, and Samuel Dunn, who had been the protagonists in a struggle against the rigid policy of the Conference, which was strangely dominated in those years by Dr. Jabez Bunting, who exercised an uncanny dictatorship over the assembly, though he would strike any one to-day as a third-rate personality.

The union of all the Methodist communities in 1932 healed all the ancient breaches, but between 1849 and 1857 Methodism lost a hundred thousand members, and, unhappily, not more than about a third of these were incorporated in the seceding community. There can be no doubt that this disastrous chapter in the history of Methodism was due to the clash between the clericalism of the Conference, backed by a conservative tendency which had grown amongst the Methodist people generally, and the liberal ideas that were abroad immediately before and after 1848, the year of revolutions.

Any attempt to estimate the social and humanitarian contribution of Methodism should not fail to take account of its cultural results in the most general range. It lifted multitudes from a life of ignorance and brutality, and (apart from all its deeper moral and religious effect upon their lives) it made them intelligent and responsible men ; it gave them some interest in books and in music, if only at first in religious books and in sacred music. Many a man who would otherwise have been a mere brute was brought, first of all, to an experience of religion, and then led to study his Bible, and to read some of the books either written by Wesley or recommended by him to his people. Very often he went on to familiarize himself with the best literature, and some of the early preachers, in particular, pursued their studies in such a way as to acquire real scholarship. Moreover, the Methodists came to know most of the hymns of the Wesleys by heart, which was in itself something of a literary discipline, and, as these hymns were sung, many a man acquired an interest in music, and in good music, for many of the tunes of early Methodism were magnificent chorales borrowed from the Moravians, many more were excellent seventeenth- and eighteenth-century English melodies, and Handel himself, as is well known, wrote settings for some of Charles Wesley's hymns. In short, Methodism gave to multitudes of ordinary Englishmen a degree of culture that they would most certainly never have acquired apart from it, at least down to the last generation or two.

These general considerations as to the cultural result of Wesley's work may remind us that it is often said that Methodism has always been deficient in the aesthetic sentiment, and that the same charge is true of Wesley himself. As regards Wesley this seems a particularly futile piece of criticism. He was a man of his century, of course, and nobody has ever claimed that he was much ahead of his age in the matter of artistic perception. But he was genuinely interested, as his *Journal* is enough to prove, not only in literature, but in music and painting and architecture. His remark about Cologne Cathedral that it was ' mere heaps upon heaps ; a huge, misshapen thing ', has been quoted many times as a proof of his insensibility to the beauty of Gothic. But, as it happens, Wesley was quite right on this occasion, and the criticism does not reflect upon his lack of taste, but upon the critic's lack of knowledge. I once bought in a street near the cathedral at Cologne a copy of an eighteenth-century print which shows the building as Wesley saw it. The choir was finished, but almost hidden by the surrounding houses ; the walls of the nave had only been carried up to about half their present height, and were covered by a squat, ugly wooden roof ; the transepts had not been built, and the wonderful spires did not exist, for the western towers were unfinished stumps. The great cathedral was then, in fact, as Wesley said, a disfigured fragment. Wesley was full of admiration for the cathedrals of England, despite the eighteenth-century dislike of Gothic. He said that he did not know whether to admire more the cathedral at Lincoln or that at York. Smollett, the novelist, who was his contemporary, much preferred the Assembly Room at York to the Minster, and said that ' the external appearance of an old Cathedral cannot but be displeasing to the eye of every man who has any idea of propriety and proportion '.

The alleged ugliness of many old chapels has been used to point the same sneer against those who followed Wesley. That is really rather brutal.

The early Methodists were poor folk, and they built out of their scanty means such sanctuaries as they could. For my own part, I always feel inclined to take off my hat to a little red-brick, red-tiled chapel in a village, when I remember how it came to be there, and what it meant, and means. Labourers who earned twelve shillings a week denied themselves of the very necessaries of life to build it ; generations of godly folk worshipped there ; many a man heard the word of God there, and repented and believed, and from that time forth lived a life full of good deeds. It may be true that there is an ancient and beautiful church in the village. Why were not the people content to go there ? If the truth must be told, because in many places the church was served by a clergyman who was merely a country gentleman, with no spiritual gifts or spiritual experience whatever, and in many others by a hard-drinking, hard-swearing, hard-riding parson whose life was a scandal to the whole neighbourhood.

But let us return to the aesthetic issue. The lack of architectural beauty in the Methodist chapels, it has been said, was partly due to poverty. No doubt it was partly due to another factor. How many beautiful buildings are there in England dating between 1738 and 1791 ? The parish churches that were built in the Georgian period are, if anything, uglier than the chapels that were built by the Methodists, because they are more pretentious, while no better in style. But no one would dream of alleging the ugliness of Georgian churches as proof positive that Anglicans are indifferent to beauty.

In short, while Methodism was a religious movement with the most spiritual aims, seeking first and last to win men from a life of sin, and bring them to the knowledge of God, it had secondary results of a very important kind. It not only helped to promote social and humanitarian reforms in many directions, but it also had a widespread cultural effect on multitudes of the English people, since, during more than a hundred years, it raised thousands of men from a state of mere ignorance and brutality, and gave them some knowledge of literature and music, to say nothing of the intellectual value of their interest in the oratory of the pulpit, and the theology of the Church.

Chapter VIII

METHODISM AND THE FUTURE

What is to be the future? If we look back upon the history of the past we see Methodism as a great revival of primitive Christianity, which evangelized England with amazing success, and spread rapidly throughout the world, for more than a hundred years after John Wesley began his work. Never since the days of the apostles had there been a spiritual movement so vital, so intense, so rapid, and so widespread. The Methodist community in this land was increasing at the rate of tens of thousands every year until its growth was checked by the disastrous disputes which took place in the middle of the last century. The wounds of that sad period have been happily healed, and the union of all the Methodists in this land is an accomplished fact. Will Methodism now resume its triumphant march, and evangelize this country afresh?

The answer to that question depends upon another. Can Methodism recover its own proper genius, and therefore be able, in the providence of God, to do its own proper work? It all depends upon Methodism returning upon itself, and regaining the spirit of the early days. We need, above all things, to ' recapture That first, fine careless rapture '.

But any consideration of the future of Methodism will raise in the minds of many people the question

of the reunion of the Churches. Will there be in
the future a union of the Evangelical Free Churches
in this country, like that which has been accomplished in Canada ? or will there be some still
larger union ? or will the Churches maintain (and
possibly accentuate) their separate characteristics,
and nevertheless (let us hope) learn to work together amicably, under some scheme of federation,
for the extension of the Kingdom of God ?

I cannot conceal my own conviction that the
whole conception of reunion, as it is commonly
envisaged and discussed, is beset with fallacies.
The most serious of these is that spiritual unity is
continually confused with organic union. Yet the
two things are obviously quite different. There is
more spiritual unity between, say, Methodists and
Congregationalists, though they belong to separate
ecclesiastical organizations, than there is between
Low Churchmen and High Churchmen in the
Church of England, though they belong to the same
ecclesiastical organization, for the Low Churchman
may be as near to the Plymouth Brethren in his
religious convictions as the High Churchman is to
the Roman Catholics, while the Methodist and the
Congregationalist may hold substantially the same
views of evangelical religion. Thus there may be,
and there is, as a matter of fact, more unity of spirit
– a greater identity of religious experience and
religious conviction, and a greater readiness to work
together – as between some Christians who are
organized into separate communities, than between
others who belong to the same community. Union
in the sense of a single, solid, uniform organization
is manifestly one thing, and union in the sense of
a spiritual unity, a community of faith and fellowship and love, is manifestly another. Yet the two
things are perpetually confused. Our Lord's

prayer ' that they all may be one ' is constantly quoted, as if it meant His desire that all His followers in the world should belong to a single organization – an interpretation that we may be sure was far from His thoughts and far below His wishes.

Moreover, to speak of the reunion of the Churches is to use a question-begging epithet, for it implies that the Church was once a single organization, that the unity of that organization has been broken up, and that it is desirable that this organic union should be now restored. But the Church of Christ never was a single organization in the sense supposed. In the earliest age there were scattered groups of believers here and there, without any common bond of organization whatever : the unity consisted in the fact that all who called themselves by the name of Christ throughout the world acknowledged one another as brethren, and loved and helped one another. It was in fact a spiritual unity : a oneness in faith and fellowship. There was no supreme ecclesiastical authority, and there was no uniform ecclesiastical organization.

It is a singular paradox in the history of the Church that the very attempt to introduce organic union brought disunion. For it was when episcopal government developed, and when the Bishops of Constantinople and Rome – the actual capital and the traditional capital of the Empire – managed to extend their authority over the churches in the districts around, that the Church crystallized, not into one organization, but into two, the Church of the East and the Church of the West, which have seldom been at peace with each other through the centuries.

Reunion is, therefore, a delusive phrase. But whether we speak of reunion or of union (which may be a very dubious blessing, whatever it is called), or of that unity of spirit, that oneness in faith and fellowship and love and service, which is most passionately to be desired and sought, the question of the future of Methodism remains very much the same, as far as essentials are concerned. For in any case it is surely unthinkable that the witness and the spirit of Methodism should disappear and be lost. Even in the metallic uniformity of the Roman Catholic Church there has managed to survive something of a distinct tradition of devotion and of service among the Benedictines, the Franciscans, the Dominicans, and the Jesuits, and even in an absolute fusion of all the Christian communities in the world (if such a thing were possible, to say nothing as to whether it is desirable or otherwise) one would expect to see Methodists surviving as a distinct order, with their own witness and their own tradition steadily maintained. Anything less than that would mean a real impoverishment of historic Christianity, and a definite loss to the Church of God.

But, to return from speculations that are remote, and perhaps fantastic, it is quite certain that Methodism will only survive in any form, and will only do the work that it is meant to do, in the providence of God, as it is true to itself. For the space of a life-time past Methodism has hardly been true to itself, because it has been uncertain of itself. Many Methodists seem to have been suffering from what it is fashionable to call, in the psychological jargon of the day, an inferiority complex. There is a great deal of odd and minute evidence as to this attitude. If some kindly bishop has conceded that John Wesley was a great man, or some literary critic has admitted that Charles Wesley wrote some fine hymns, or an historian has declared that Methodism was a remarkable movement in English religion, the utterance has been reverently quoted and made much of – as if the Wesleys needed a patronizing word from men immeasurably smaller than themselves, and as if Methodism did not stand out for all to see as the greatest thing that has happened in the religious world since the Reformation ! Our people do not seem latterly to have realized, in the way their fathers did, the greatness of our Methodist history and heritage and mission. They have been a little ashamed of what was really characteristic. They have tried to assimilate themselves to other standards, and have readily abandoned their own *differentia*. They have been very anxious to show that they are really as cultured and as modern as anybody else, and not in the least fanatical or extreme.

Take our attitude to the great hymns of Methodism, which are a priceless part of our inheritance. In the past those hymns were our devotional and experimental standard. They expressed and safeguarded the norm of Methodist experience, and helped to re-create it from generation to generation, because they were in constant use both in public worship and in private devotion. When I began to preach, as a lad in my 'teens, I used to be deeply impressed, again and again, when I heard the prayers of the Lincolnshire peasants in those village chapels, and not only by the depth of the spiritual experience that was expressed, but by the beauty of the imagery and the dignity of the language that were used to express it. Now, many of those agricultural labourers had never earned more than fifteen shillings a week, and had never seen more than three or four books, in all their lives. But there was a grandeur of thought and a chastity of language in their prayers that was astonishing. The reason was, of course, that they knew by heart

much of the Bible, and most of the hymns of the
Wesleys, and they found there the secret both of a
deep experience and of a language that was stately
and beautiful. That kind of spiritual culture has
largely died out since those days. There have been
many Methodist services of late years where not a
single Methodist hymn has been used, and the
people have been allowed to sing nothing but the
feeble and sentimental verses of modern English
and American poetasters. There is something
faulty both in our literary and our spiritual insight
if we really like this sort of thing better than the
great hymns of Charles Wesley, with their profoundly evangelical and mystical spirit, to say
nothing of their lyrical quality. Behind all this
sort of preference there is a subtle distrust of the
paradox and the passion of the evangelical experience at its best, which was so characteristic of real
Methodism in the past.

Again, we have allowed many of our characteristic institutions to perish. We have multiplied all
sorts of organizations in imitation of those possessed
by other Churches, but the Band Meeting has
gone ; the Lovefeast has practically disappeared,
though it was one of our most definite revivals of
the usages of the primitive Church ; and the
Covenant Service has been tinkered with until
nearly all its searching and impressive character
has been lost. The Class Meeting has gone in many
places, and that is the most serious loss of all.[1] If

---

[1] After the appearance of the Rev. Matthieu Lelièvre's *John Wesley, sa
vie et son oeuvre*, Charles de Rémusat wrote an article in the *Revue des Deux
Mondes* (for January 1870) entitled *Wesley et le Méthodisme*. Commenting on
the division of the Society into Classes and Bands, in the early days, he says,
with real insight : ' Ces classifications, simplifiées depuis, maintenaient le
principe qui a subsisté et qui a fait la force et la durée du méthodisme, celui
de la vie commune des âmes ou la recherche en commun de la rédemption
par la réunion et la solidarité des fideles, formant ce que Spener avait
appelé *ecclesiolae in ecclesia*.'

any one suggests it had lost its use and value, I simply deny that. Forty odd years ago, in a Class Meeting of the traditional type, I learned more of the sheer realities of religion than I have ever learned anywhere else, before or since, and there are some Class Meetings surviving to-day that are doing the same invaluable service for young folk. The Watchnight is almost the only distinctively Methodist service that has survived, and it has managed to endure because it has been adopted by other Churches. All the way through it is evident that for a generation or two past we have been nervous about anything that is distinctively Method-ist, and have only been reassured as to the retention of anything in our special tradition when it has been endorsed and adopted by somebody else – then we have dared to maintain it.

There is no great future for Methodism if it becomes characterless and colourless, and practic-ally indistinguishable from the other evangelical communities. But there is a great future for it if it will be faithful to its own peculiar genius. If we have nothing in particular of any value to contribute to religion to-day, we have no excuse for existence. But if we have an experience, a message, a mission, that is peculiarly our own, a witness that we can bear, and a work that we can do, better than any one else, then there is still a place for us. For my own part, I am sure that we have a special mission and a special message, and I am jealous lest we should forget it, as we seem to have been tending to do.

The trite counsel, ' To thine own self be true ', is as necessary for an institution as it is for a person. It is only when a movement is true to itself that it retains any real energy and vitality ; it is only when a community is true to itself that it has either

the power to grow or, indeed, the right to exist.
That seems perfectly obvious. How much longer
would the Conservative Party survive, for example,
if it became a pale copy of the Labour Party, or
the Shakespeare Society if it lost all interest in our
Elizabethan literature? It is only when a group
maintains a special faith, a special witness, a special
mission, that it can continue to function. If we as
Methodists have nothing unique to contribute to
religious life, and if our whole message is being
delivered effectively by, say, Anglicans or Congregationalists, why should we persist? Have we not
some special evangelical emphasis, some particular
evangelistic note, which belongs peculiarly to us,
and which nobody else can stress so well? We had,
and we still have, if we are only true to our own
tradition.

Every new development in thought or experience
has its real source in the past. Early Methodism
was a revival of evangelical truth and evangelical
experience, going back to the Reformation and the
apostolic age. The human spirit is always renewed
by some creative contact with the past, as the
strength of Antaeus was renewed whenever he fell
back upon the earth, which was his mother. It is
always so. There is never an absolutely new depar-
ture. However novel, however adventurous, however unexpected a new movement is, if it has any
real promise for the future, it derives in some way
from the past. A real revival of Methodism can
only come by way of a rediscovery and a recapture
of the essential witness of early Methodism. What
was most vital in that witness? There cannot be
much doubt as to the answer. Early Methodism
witnessed to the experience of assurance – that is to
say, a present and personal certainty of religious experience. All that is really vital and characteristic

in Methodism follows from that personal experience of assurance. That is the deep secret of spiritual joy. You cannot rejoice over a dubious experience and an uncertain hope. You must be sure of anything before you can be really glad about it. The characteristic Methodist experience was one of joy because it was one of certainty. One of the most remarkable characteristics of the literature of early Methodism is the sense of joy and rapture and triumph that appears so constantly, and here the parallel with the New Testament is very striking. There, too, is heard the accent of a new and strange and unearthly happiness : the first Christians rejoiced with a joy that was unspeakable, and full of glory.

Similarly, the need and the desire for fellowship, in its more intimate forms, follows upon the experience of assurance. It has always been the mark of this type of religious experience that it has sought fellowship, and the very reality of fellowship, in the only way it can be found – that is to say, in the device of groups. There are few things more suggestive than that in the history of the Church. In the primitive days the group existed because each small Christian community *was* a group. It was re-created both in the monasticism and in the mystical sects of the Middle Ages. It was re-created again in Pietism, and in Moravianism, and in Methodism, and now once more in the Oxford Group Movement. There is a kind of fellowship, of course, in merely belonging to a Church, and a more intimate fellowship around the Lord's Table, but the closest intimacy of fellowship is impossible among a hundred people ; it must be sought in the group of a dozen or so. That was the vital fact in the Society Classes.

Again, it is the experience of assurance that

makes real evangelism. You do not passionately proclaim that of which you are not quite certain. It is only when you are humbly and happily sure of salvation yourself that you can offer it to others in no uncertain voice. Only then can you say, ' O let me commend *my* Saviour to *you* ! '

What evangelistic activity still survives among us has been very largely segregated and departmentalized. There was a time when every Methodist witnessed to the saving grace of God, by word and deed ; when every Methodist preacher had an evangelistic message, and sought week by week very definitely to bring men to decision for Christ ; when every Methodist congregation was a centre of many kinds of evangelistic activity – there was visiting from house to house with religious appeals ; there were meetings for prayer and fellowship not only in the church, but in private dwellings, where the neighbours were invited to attend ; there was preaching out of doors, and so on. There is little of all this to-day, alas ! Instead, we have missions and missioners. Some ministers and some laymen are set apart to visit the various churches from time to time, and hold missions, a series of special services, lasting for a week or two. Such a mission may be held once every few years, and in between there may be no very definite evangelistic work at all. Moreover, in all the large towns there are Central Halls which are known as missions, and there is a marked tendency for the other Methodist churches in the place to leave the evangelistic enterprise to these institutions. The change that has come about is like the difference between the early period of human life, when every man in the tribe was a warrior, and the later days, when a nation committed the business of war to a profes-

sional army. There may be very good reason for
having a special class of preachers known as missioners and a special class of churches known as
missions, but there is no excuse whatever for leaving
the evangelistic work of the Church to these agents
and these centres. If any community of Methodists
ceases to be aggressive in the work of seeking the
salvation of men it betrays its whole history and
character and purpose.

Moreover, in such evangelistic activity as there
has been in Methodism during the last generation
or two there has been one deep defect. When we
have sought from time to time to bring people to
spiritual decision in special services and periodical
missions, the method has been to ask for some token
of decision such as lifting a hand, standing up, or
signing a card. I am not despising any of these
things. Decision is a vital fact, and it is important
that it should be signified and registered in some
definite way. But decision is not the whole of the
initial experience in the soul's life. When I make
up my mind to yield to Christ, that is not all that
there is to be done or to be experienced. I ought
to go on to seek what the Apostle called the witness
of the Spirit, a God-given assurance that I am forgiven and accepted of God. That is the privilege
of every penitent and believing soul, and we ought
to urge those who profess decision to seek that
definite experience of spiritual certainty, and to
seek it until they find it.

We ought to preach that message of assurance
continually. That is only to say, in effect, that our
preaching ought to range steadily within the orbit
of a real gospel, that it ought to deal directly and
continually with sin and salvation, the need of man
and the grace of God, the deep wants of the human
soul and the marvellous redemption that is in

Christ, and all with the purpose of effecting an experience of those great facts in the soul. There can be no religious experience worth the name unless we really feel our need of deliverance from sin and self ; there can be no religious experience of the highest kind unless we really feel as assured of our salvation as we were of our need. Any kind of preaching that leaves a general impression behind that there is nothing seriously wrong with humanity, and therefore no need for any very definite experience of renewal, or, for the matter of that, for any unique and unutterable deed of redemption in Christ, is falling far short of the essential gospel. The need of man is tragic, and the salvation of God is wonderful. The effect of our preaching ought to be to create in the penitent and believing heart that miraculous experience of spiritual renewal which brings with it the sense of wonder and certainty and joy.

There is still, thank God ! a sound core of real evangelical experience in the Methodist people. The most cheering thing I know about Methodism is the wonderful way that our people still respond to the plain, direct, urgent, passionate preaching of a real gospel of salvation. The response is not only among the old saints ; one would expect that, because they have a real experience, but it is also very strikingly among the young people, because some of them have a real experience, and many more of them feel their need of it.

I am deeply convinced that what Methodism needs to-day more than anything else is to be re-called to itself. We need to realize afresh our own heritage, our own tradition, our own mission. If we can recover the sense of wonder and joy which so marvellously characterized the early Method-ists, and which sprang, like their evangelism and their fellowship, out of the deep certainty of a real experience of the redeeming love of God in Christ, then there is still a great future of service and of blessedness for ' the People called Methodists '.

INDEX

251